50 High-Protein Mediterranean Salad Recipes for Home

By: Kelly Johnson

Table of Contents

- Greek Quinoa Salad with Chickpeas
- Grilled Chicken and Feta Salad
- Lentil and Roasted Vegetable Salad
- Tuna and White Bean Salad
- Mediterranean Couscous Salad with Grilled Shrimp
- Greek Salad with Grilled Salmon
- Chickpea and Roasted Red Pepper Salad
- Turkey and Quinoa Tabouli Salad
- Grilled Steak and Vegetable Salad
- Greek Orzo Salad with Grilled Chicken
- Mediterranean Tofu Salad with Olives
- Shrimp and Avocado Salad with Feta
- Mediterranean Three Bean Salad
- Chicken and Farro Salad with Sun-Dried Tomatoes
- Greek Pasta Salad with Chicken
- Quinoa and Black Bean Salad with Avocado
- Grilled Lamb and Couscous Salad
- Mediterranean Eggplant and Chickpea Salad
- Turkey and Bulgur Salad with Pistachios
- Greek Yogurt Chicken Salad
- Lentil and Tuna Salad with Capers
- Mediterranean Cauliflower Salad with Tahini Dressing
- Grilled Swordfish and White Bean Salad
- Greek Spinach Salad with Grilled Halloumi
- Quinoa and Edamame Salad with Lemon Vinaigrette
- Mediterranean Zucchini Ribbon Salad with Pine Nuts
- Chicken and White Bean Salad with Pesto
- Greek Kale Salad with Quinoa and Cranberries
- Lentil and Chicken Salad with Yogurt Dressing
- Mediterranean Chickpea and Tomato Salad
- Grilled Turkey and Vegetable Salad with Feta
- Greek-style Salmon Salad with Orzo
- Quinoa and Roasted Vegetable Salad with Balsamic Glaze
- Mediterranean Bean Salad with Tuna
- Greek Lentil Salad with Feta

- Grilled Chicken and Eggplant Salad
- Mediterranean Bulgur Salad with Grilled Shrimp
- Greek-style Beef and Olive Salad
- Quinoa and Avocado Salad with Lemon-Tahini Dressing
- Mediterranean Cucumber Salad with Yogurt Dressing
- Chicken and Artichoke Salad with White Beans
- Greek-style Pork and Olive Salad
- Lentil and Salmon Salad with Dill Dressing
- Mediterranean Barley Salad with Grilled Vegetables
- Greek-style Turkey and Quinoa Salad
- Quinoa and Chickpea Salad with Roasted Red Pepper Dressing
- Mediterranean Roasted Beet Salad with Goat Cheese
- Grilled Tofu and Vegetable Salad with Feta
- Greek-style Chicken and Pasta Salad
- Lentil and Tofu Salad with Lemon-Tahini Dressing

Greek Quinoa Salad with Chickpeas

Ingredients:

- 1 cup quinoa, rinsed
- 2 cups water or vegetable broth
- 1 can (15 ounces) chickpeas, drained and rinsed
- 1 cucumber, diced
- 1 cup cherry tomatoes, halved
- 1/2 red onion, finely chopped
- 1/2 cup Kalamata olives, pitted and sliced
- 1/2 cup crumbled feta cheese
- 1/4 cup chopped fresh parsley
- 1/4 cup chopped fresh mint
- 1/4 cup extra virgin olive oil
- 2 tablespoons lemon juice
- 1 clove garlic, minced
- Salt and pepper to taste

Instructions:

1. In a medium saucepan, combine the quinoa and water or vegetable broth. Bring to a boil, then reduce the heat to low. Cover and simmer for 15-20 minutes, or until the quinoa is cooked and the liquid is absorbed. Remove from heat and let it cool.
2. In a large mixing bowl, combine the cooked quinoa, chickpeas, cucumber, cherry tomatoes, red onion, Kalamata olives, feta cheese, parsley, and mint.
3. In a small bowl, whisk together the olive oil, lemon juice, minced garlic, salt, and pepper to make the dressing.
4. Pour the dressing over the salad ingredients in the mixing bowl. Toss gently until everything is evenly coated with the dressing.
5. Taste and adjust seasoning if needed. You can add more salt, pepper, or lemon juice according to your preference.
6. Serve immediately or chill in the refrigerator for at least 30 minutes to allow the flavors to meld together before serving.
7. Enjoy your Greek Quinoa Salad with Chickpeas as a nutritious and satisfying meal or side dish!

Grilled Chicken and Feta Salad

Ingredients:

For the Grilled Chicken:

- 2 boneless, skinless chicken breasts
- 2 tablespoons olive oil
- 1 tablespoon lemon juice
- 2 cloves garlic, minced
- 1 teaspoon dried oregano
- Salt and pepper to taste

For the Salad:

- 6 cups mixed salad greens (such as lettuce, spinach, arugula)
- 1 cucumber, sliced
- 1 cup cherry tomatoes, halved
- 1/2 red onion, thinly sliced
- 1/2 cup Kalamata olives, pitted
- 1/2 cup crumbled feta cheese
- 1/4 cup chopped fresh parsley
- 2 tablespoons extra virgin olive oil
- 1 tablespoon red wine vinegar
- Salt and pepper to taste

Instructions:

1. In a bowl, whisk together olive oil, lemon juice, minced garlic, dried oregano, salt, and pepper. Place the chicken breasts in a shallow dish or a resealable plastic bag and pour the marinade over them. Make sure the chicken is evenly coated. Marinate in the refrigerator for at least 30 minutes, or up to 4 hours.
2. Preheat your grill to medium-high heat. Remove the chicken from the marinade and discard any excess marinade. Grill the chicken breasts for 6-8 minutes per side, or until they are cooked through and no longer pink in the center. Remove from the grill and let them rest for a few minutes before slicing.

3. While the chicken is grilling, prepare the salad ingredients. In a large salad bowl, combine the mixed salad greens, sliced cucumber, cherry tomatoes, red onion, Kalamata olives, crumbled feta cheese, and chopped fresh parsley.
4. In a small bowl, whisk together extra virgin olive oil, red wine vinegar, salt, and pepper to make the salad dressing.
5. Once the chicken has rested, slice it into thin strips.
6. Add the sliced grilled chicken to the salad bowl.
7. Drizzle the salad dressing over the salad ingredients and toss gently to coat everything evenly with the dressing.
8. Taste and adjust seasoning if needed.
9. Serve immediately, garnished with additional parsley if desired.
10. Enjoy your Grilled Chicken and Feta Salad as a delicious and nutritious meal!

Lentil and Roasted Vegetable Salad

Ingredients:

For the Roasted Vegetables:

- 2 cups diced vegetables (such as bell peppers, zucchini, eggplant, carrots)
- 2 tablespoons olive oil
- 1 teaspoon dried thyme
- Salt and pepper to taste

For the Lentils:

- 1 cup dry green or brown lentils
- 3 cups water or vegetable broth
- 1 bay leaf
- Salt to taste

For the Salad:

- Roasted vegetables (from above)
- Cooked lentils (from above)
- 1/2 cup cherry tomatoes, halved
- 1/4 cup chopped red onion
- 1/4 cup chopped fresh parsley
- 1/4 cup crumbled feta cheese (optional)
- 2 tablespoons extra virgin olive oil
- 2 tablespoons balsamic vinegar
- Salt and pepper to taste

Instructions:

1. Preheat your oven to 400°F (200°C). Line a baking sheet with parchment paper or lightly grease it.
2. In a bowl, toss the diced vegetables with olive oil, dried thyme, salt, and pepper until evenly coated. Spread them out in a single layer on the prepared baking sheet.

3. Roast the vegetables in the preheated oven for 20-25 minutes, or until they are tender and lightly browned, stirring halfway through cooking. Once done, remove from the oven and let them cool slightly.
4. While the vegetables are roasting, rinse the lentils under cold water and drain them.
5. In a medium saucepan, combine the lentils, water or vegetable broth, and bay leaf. Bring to a boil over medium-high heat, then reduce the heat to low and simmer for 20-25 minutes, or until the lentils are tender but still hold their shape. Remove from heat, discard the bay leaf, and drain any excess liquid. Season with salt to taste.
6. In a large salad bowl, combine the cooked lentils, roasted vegetables, cherry tomatoes, chopped red onion, and chopped fresh parsley. If using, add the crumbled feta cheese.
7. In a small bowl, whisk together the extra virgin olive oil and balsamic vinegar to make the dressing. Season with salt and pepper to taste.
8. Drizzle the dressing over the salad ingredients in the bowl and toss gently to coat everything evenly with the dressing.
9. Taste and adjust seasoning if needed.
10. Serve the Lentil and Roasted Vegetable Salad immediately, or chill it in the refrigerator for at least 30 minutes before serving to allow the flavors to meld together.
11. Enjoy your delicious and nutritious Lentil and Roasted Vegetable Salad as a meal or side dish!

Tuna and White Bean Salad

Ingredients:

- 2 cans (5 ounces each) of tuna, drained
- 2 cans (15 ounces each) of white beans (such as cannelini beans), drained and rinsed
- 1/2 red onion, finely chopped
- 1/2 cup chopped fresh parsley
- 1/4 cup chopped fresh basil
- 1/4 cup chopped fresh dill
- 1/4 cup extra virgin olive oil
- 2 tablespoons red wine vinegar
- 1 tablespoon lemon juice
- 1 clove garlic, minced
- Salt and pepper to taste
- Optional: cherry tomatoes, sliced cucumber, mixed salad greens

Instructions:

1. In a large mixing bowl, combine the drained tuna, white beans, chopped red onion, chopped parsley, chopped basil, and chopped dill.
2. In a small bowl, whisk together the extra virgin olive oil, red wine vinegar, lemon juice, minced garlic, salt, and pepper to make the dressing.
3. Pour the dressing over the tuna and white bean mixture in the mixing bowl. Toss gently until everything is evenly coated with the dressing.
4. Taste and adjust seasoning if needed. You can add more salt, pepper, or lemon juice according to your preference.
5. If desired, serve the Tuna and White Bean Salad over a bed of mixed salad greens and garnish with sliced cherry tomatoes and cucumber.
6. Alternatively, you can chill the salad in the refrigerator for at least 30 minutes before serving to allow the flavors to meld together.
7. Enjoy your Tuna and White Bean Salad as a nutritious and satisfying meal or side dish!

Mediterranean Couscous Salad with Grilled Shrimp

Ingredients:

For the Grilled Shrimp:

- 1 pound large shrimp, peeled and deveined
- 2 tablespoons olive oil
- 2 cloves garlic, minced
- 1 teaspoon dried oregano
- 1/2 teaspoon paprika
- Salt and pepper to taste

For the Couscous Salad:

- 1 cup couscous
- 1 1/4 cups vegetable broth or water
- 1 cup cherry tomatoes, halved
- 1 cucumber, diced
- 1/2 red onion, finely chopped
- 1/2 cup Kalamata olives, pitted and sliced
- 1/4 cup chopped fresh parsley
- 1/4 cup chopped fresh mint
- 1/4 cup crumbled feta cheese (optional)
- 2 tablespoons extra virgin olive oil
- 2 tablespoons lemon juice
- Salt and pepper to taste

Instructions:

1. Preheat your grill to medium-high heat.
2. In a bowl, combine the peeled and deveined shrimp with olive oil, minced garlic, dried oregano, paprika, salt, and pepper. Toss until the shrimp are evenly coated with the marinade.

3. Thread the marinated shrimp onto skewers. If you're using wooden skewers, make sure to soak them in water for about 30 minutes beforehand to prevent them from burning on the grill.
4. Grill the shrimp skewers for 2-3 minutes per side, or until they are pink and opaque. Remove from the grill and set aside.
5. While the shrimp are grilling, prepare the couscous according to the package instructions. Typically, you'll bring the vegetable broth or water to a boil, then stir in the couscous, cover, and remove from heat. Let it sit for 5 minutes, then fluff it with a fork.
6. In a large mixing bowl, combine the cooked couscous, halved cherry tomatoes, diced cucumber, finely chopped red onion, sliced Kalamata olives, chopped fresh parsley, and chopped fresh mint. If using, add the crumbled feta cheese.
7. In a small bowl, whisk together the extra virgin olive oil and lemon juice to make the dressing. Season with salt and pepper to taste.
8. Pour the dressing over the couscous salad ingredients in the mixing bowl. Toss gently until everything is evenly coated with the dressing.
9. Taste and adjust seasoning if needed.
10. Serve the Mediterranean Couscous Salad with Grilled Shrimp, placing the grilled shrimp skewers on top of the salad or on the side.
11. Enjoy your flavorful and satisfying Mediterranean meal!

Greek Salad with Grilled Salmon

Ingredients:

For the Grilled Salmon:

- 4 salmon fillets (6 ounces each), skin-on
- 2 tablespoons olive oil
- 1 tablespoon lemon juice
- 2 cloves garlic, minced
- 1 teaspoon dried oregano
- Salt and pepper to taste

For the Greek Salad:

- 4 cups mixed salad greens (such as lettuce, spinach, arugula)
- 1 cucumber, diced
- 1 cup cherry tomatoes, halved
- 1/2 red onion, thinly sliced
- 1/2 cup Kalamata olives, pitted
- 1/2 cup crumbled feta cheese
- 1/4 cup chopped fresh parsley
- 2 tablespoons extra virgin olive oil
- 1 tablespoon red wine vinegar
- Salt and pepper to taste
- Optional: lemon wedges for serving

Instructions:

1. Preheat your grill to medium-high heat.
2. In a bowl, whisk together olive oil, lemon juice, minced garlic, dried oregano, salt, and pepper. Place the salmon fillets in a shallow dish or a resealable plastic bag and pour the marinade over them. Make sure the salmon is evenly coated. Marinate in the refrigerator for at least 30 minutes, or up to 1 hour.
3. While the salmon is marinating, prepare the Greek salad ingredients. In a large salad bowl, combine the mixed salad greens, diced cucumber, halved cherry

tomatoes, thinly sliced red onion, pitted Kalamata olives, crumbled feta cheese, and chopped fresh parsley.
4. In a small bowl, whisk together extra virgin olive oil, red wine vinegar, salt, and pepper to make the salad dressing.
5. Once the grill is preheated, remove the salmon fillets from the marinade and discard any excess marinade. Place the salmon fillets skin-side down on the grill. Grill for 4-5 minutes per side, or until the salmon is cooked through and flakes easily with a fork. Remove from the grill and let them rest for a few minutes.
6. While the salmon is resting, drizzle the salad dressing over the Greek salad ingredients in the bowl. Toss gently to coat everything evenly with the dressing.
7. Divide the Greek salad among serving plates.
8. Place a grilled salmon fillet on top of each serving of Greek salad.
9. Optionally, serve with lemon wedges on the side for squeezing over the salmon.
10. Enjoy your delicious and nutritious Greek Salad with Grilled Salmon!

Chickpea and Roasted Red Pepper Salad

Ingredients:

- 2 cans (15 ounces each) chickpeas, drained and rinsed
- 2 roasted red peppers, chopped (you can use jarred roasted red peppers or roast your own)
- 1/2 red onion, finely chopped
- 1/4 cup chopped fresh parsley
- 1/4 cup chopped fresh basil
- 1/4 cup crumbled feta cheese (optional)
- 2 tablespoons extra virgin olive oil
- 1 tablespoon red wine vinegar
- 1 clove garlic, minced
- Salt and pepper to taste

Instructions:

1. In a large mixing bowl, combine the drained and rinsed chickpeas, chopped roasted red peppers, finely chopped red onion, chopped fresh parsley, and chopped fresh basil.
2. If using, add the crumbled feta cheese to the bowl.
3. In a small bowl, whisk together the extra virgin olive oil, red wine vinegar, minced garlic, salt, and pepper to make the dressing.
4. Pour the dressing over the chickpea and roasted red pepper mixture in the large mixing bowl. Toss gently until everything is evenly coated with the dressing.
5. Taste and adjust seasoning if needed. You can add more salt, pepper, or vinegar according to your preference.
6. Serve the Chickpea and Roasted Red Pepper Salad immediately, or chill it in the refrigerator for at least 30 minutes before serving to allow the flavors to meld together.
7. Enjoy your flavorful and nutritious salad as a side dish or a light meal!

Turkey and Quinoa Tabouli Salad

Ingredients:

For the Salad:

- 1 cup quinoa, rinsed
- 2 cups water or vegetable broth
- 1 pound ground turkey
- 2 tablespoons olive oil
- 2 cloves garlic, minced
- 1 teaspoon ground cumin
- 1/2 teaspoon paprika
- Salt and pepper to taste
- 1 cucumber, diced
- 1 cup cherry tomatoes, halved
- 1/2 red onion, finely chopped
- 1/4 cup chopped fresh parsley
- 1/4 cup chopped fresh mint
- 1/4 cup crumbled feta cheese (optional)
- Lemon wedges for serving

For the Dressing:

- 1/4 cup extra virgin olive oil
- 2 tablespoons lemon juice
- 1 clove garlic, minced
- Salt and pepper to taste

Instructions:

1. In a medium saucepan, combine the quinoa and water or vegetable broth. Bring to a boil, then reduce the heat to low. Cover and simmer for 15-20 minutes, or until the quinoa is cooked and the liquid is absorbed. Remove from heat and let it cool.

2. In a large skillet, heat 1 tablespoon of olive oil over medium heat. Add the minced garlic and cook for 1 minute until fragrant.
3. Add the ground turkey to the skillet, breaking it apart with a spatula. Cook until the turkey is browned and cooked through, about 5-7 minutes. Season with ground cumin, paprika, salt, and pepper. Remove from heat and set aside.
4. In a large mixing bowl, combine the cooked quinoa, cooked ground turkey, diced cucumber, halved cherry tomatoes, finely chopped red onion, chopped fresh parsley, and chopped fresh mint. If using, add the crumbled feta cheese.
5. In a small bowl, whisk together the extra virgin olive oil, lemon juice, minced garlic, salt, and pepper to make the dressing.
6. Pour the dressing over the salad ingredients in the mixing bowl. Toss gently until everything is evenly coated with the dressing.
7. Taste and adjust seasoning if needed. Add more salt, pepper, or lemon juice according to your preference.
8. Serve the Turkey and Quinoa Tabouli Salad with lemon wedges on the side for squeezing over the salad.
9. Enjoy your flavorful and nutritious salad as a main dish or side dish!

Grilled Steak and Vegetable Salad

Ingredients:

For the Steak:

- 1 pound steak (such as sirloin, flank, or ribeye)
- 2 tablespoons olive oil
- 2 cloves garlic, minced
- 1 teaspoon dried thyme
- Salt and pepper to taste

For the Salad:

- 4 cups mixed salad greens (such as lettuce, spinach, arugula)
- 1 bell pepper, sliced
- 1 zucchini, sliced
- 1 red onion, sliced
- 1 cup cherry tomatoes, halved
- 1/4 cup crumbled feta cheese (optional)
- 2 tablespoons extra virgin olive oil
- 1 tablespoon balsamic vinegar
- Salt and pepper to taste

Instructions:

1. Preheat your grill to medium-high heat.
2. In a bowl, combine the olive oil, minced garlic, dried thyme, salt, and pepper. Place the steak in a shallow dish or a resealable plastic bag and pour the marinade over it. Make sure the steak is evenly coated. Marinate in the refrigerator for at least 30 minutes, or up to 2 hours.
3. While the steak is marinating, prepare the vegetables. Toss the sliced bell pepper, zucchini, and red onion with a drizzle of olive oil, salt and pepper.
4. Once the grill is preheated, remove the steak from the marinade and discard any excess marinade. Place the steak on the grill and cook to your desired level of

doneness, flipping halfway through cooking. Cooking times will vary depending on the thickness of the steak and your preferred level of doneness. As a general guideline, cook for about 4-5 minutes per side for medium-rare.
5. While the steak is grilling, grill the prepared vegetables until they are tender and slightly charred, about 3-4 minutes per side. Remove from the grill and set aside.
6. Let the grilled steak rest for a few minutes before slicing it thinly against the grain.
7. In a large salad bowl, combine the mixed salad greens, grilled vegetables, halved cherry tomatoes, and crumbled feta cheese.
8. In a small bowl, whisk together the extra virgin olive oil and balsamic vinegar to make the dressing. Season with salt and pepper to taste.
9. Drizzle the dressing over the salad ingredients in the bowl. Toss gently until everything is evenly coated with the dressing.
10. Arrange the sliced grilled steak on top of the salad.
11. Serve immediately, and enjoy your delicious Grilled Steak and Vegetable Salad!

Greek Orzo Salad with Grilled Chicken

Ingredients:

For the Grilled Chicken:

- 2 boneless, skinless chicken breasts
- 2 tablespoons olive oil
- 1 tablespoon lemon juice
- 2 cloves garlic, minced
- 1 teaspoon dried oregano
- Salt and pepper to taste

For the Orzo Salad:

- 1 cup orzo pasta
- 2 cups water or chicken broth
- 1 cucumber, diced
- 1 cup cherry tomatoes, halved
- 1/2 red onion, finely chopped
- 1/2 cup Kalamata olives, pitted and sliced
- 1/2 cup crumbled feta cheese
- 1/4 cup chopped fresh parsley
- 1/4 cup chopped fresh mint
- 2 tablespoons extra virgin olive oil
- 2 tablespoons red wine vinegar
- Salt and pepper to taste
- Optional: lemon wedges for serving

Instructions:

1. In a bowl, combine the olive oil, lemon juice, minced garlic, dried oregano, salt, and pepper. Place the chicken breasts in a shallow dish or a resealable plastic bag and pour the marinade over them. Make sure the chicken is evenly coated. Marinate in the refrigerator for at least 30 minutes, or up to 4 hours.

2. In a medium saucepan, bring the water or chicken broth to a boil. Add the orzo pasta and cook according to the package instructions, usually about 8-10 minutes, or until al dente. Drain the orzo and rinse it under cold water to stop the cooking process. Let it cool.
3. Preheat your grill to medium-high heat. Remove the chicken breasts from the marinade and discard any excess marinade. Grill the chicken breasts for 6-8 minutes per side, or until they are cooked through and no longer pink in the center. Remove from the grill and let them rest for a few minutes before slicing.
4. In a large mixing bowl, combine the cooked and cooled orzo pasta, diced cucumber, halved cherry tomatoes, finely chopped red onion, sliced Kalamata olives, crumbled feta cheese, chopped fresh parsley, and chopped fresh mint.
5. In a small bowl, whisk together the extra virgin olive oil and red wine vinegar to make the dressing. Season with salt and pepper to taste.
6. Pour the dressing over the orzo salad ingredients in the mixing bowl. Toss gently until everything is evenly coated with the dressing.
7. Taste and adjust seasoning if needed.
8. Slice the grilled chicken breasts into thin strips.
9. Serve the Greek Orzo Salad in individual bowls or plates, topping each serving with the sliced grilled chicken.
10. Optionally, serve with lemon wedges on the side for squeezing over the salad.
11. Enjoy your flavorful and satisfying Greek Orzo Salad with Grilled Chicken!

Mediterranean Tofu Salad with Olives

Ingredients:

For the Tofu:

- 1 block (14 ounces) extra firm tofu, drained and pressed
- 2 tablespoons olive oil
- 2 tablespoons soy sauce or tamari
- 1 tablespoon lemon juice
- 1 teaspoon dried oregano
- Salt and pepper to taste

For the Salad:

- 4 cups mixed salad greens (such as lettuce, spinach, arugula)
- 1 cucumber, diced
- 1 cup cherry tomatoes, halved
- 1/2 red onion, thinly sliced
- 1/2 cup Kalamata olives, pitted and sliced
- 1/4 cup crumbled feta cheese (optional)
- 1/4 cup chopped fresh parsley
- 2 tablespoons extra virgin olive oil
- 1 tablespoon red wine vinegar
- Salt and pepper to taste
- Optional: lemon wedges for serving

Instructions:

1. Preheat your oven to 400°F (200°C).
2. Slice the pressed tofu into cubes or strips. In a bowl, whisk together the olive oil, soy sauce or tamari, lemon juice, dried oregano, salt, and pepper. Add the tofu cubes to the bowl and toss gently to coat them evenly with the marinade.
3. Place the marinated tofu cubes on a baking sheet lined with parchment paper or lightly greased. Bake in the preheated oven for 25-30 minutes, flipping halfway through cooking, until the tofu is golden brown and crispy on the outside.

4. While the tofu is baking, prepare the salad ingredients. In a large salad bowl, combine the mixed salad greens, diced cucumber, halved cherry tomatoes, thinly sliced red onion, sliced Kalamata olives, crumbled feta cheese (if using), and chopped fresh parsley.
5. In a small bowl, whisk together the extra virgin olive oil and red wine vinegar to make the dressing. Season with salt and pepper to taste.
6. Once the tofu is done baking and slightly cooled, add it to the salad bowl.
7. Pour the dressing over the salad ingredients in the bowl. Toss gently until everything is evenly coated with the dressing.
8. Taste and adjust seasoning if needed.
9. Serve the Mediterranean Tofu Salad immediately, or chill it in the refrigerator for at least 30 minutes before serving to allow the flavors to meld together.
10. Optionally, serve with lemon wedges on the side for squeezing over the salad.
11. Enjoy your flavorful and nutritious Mediterranean Tofu Salad with Olives!

Shrimp and Avocado Salad with Feta

Ingredients:

For the Shrimp:

- 1 pound large shrimp, peeled and deveined
- 2 tablespoons olive oil
- 2 cloves garlic, minced
- 1 teaspoon paprika
- 1/2 teaspoon cumin
- Salt and pepper to taste

For the Salad:

- 4 cups mixed salad greens (such as lettuce, spinach, arugula)
- 2 ripe avocados, diced
- 1 cup cherry tomatoes, halved
- 1/2 red onion, thinly sliced
- 1/2 cup crumbled feta cheese
- 1/4 cup chopped fresh cilantro or parsley
- Optional: lemon wedges for serving

For the Dressing:

- 3 tablespoons extra virgin olive oil
- 2 tablespoons lime juice
- 1 clove garlic, minced
- Salt and pepper to taste

Instructions:

1. In a bowl, combine the olive oil, minced garlic, paprika, cumin, salt, and pepper. Add the peeled and deveined shrimp to the bowl and toss until they are evenly coated with the marinade. Let them marinate for about 15-30 minutes.

2. Preheat a grill or grill pan over medium-high heat. Once hot, add the marinated shrimp to the grill. Cook for about 2-3 minutes per side, or until they are pink and opaque. Remove from the grill and set aside.
3. In a large salad bowl, combine the mixed salad greens, diced avocado, halved cherry tomatoes, thinly sliced red onion, crumbled feta cheese, and chopped fresh cilantro or parsley.
4. In a small bowl, whisk together the extra virgin olive oil, lime juice, minced garlic, salt, and pepper to make the dressing.
5. Pour the dressing over the salad ingredients in the bowl. Toss gently until everything is evenly coated with the dressing.
6. Divide the salad among serving plates.
7. Top each serving with the grilled shrimp.
8. Optionally, serve with lemon wedges on the side for squeezing over the salad.
9. Enjoy your refreshing and flavorful Shrimp and Avocado Salad with Feta!

Mediterranean Three Bean Salad

Ingredients:

- 1 can (15 ounces) chickpeas, drained and rinsed
- 1 can (15 ounces) kidney beans, drained and rinsed
- 1 can (15 ounces) cannellini beans, drained and rinsed
- 1/2 red onion, finely chopped
- 1/2 cup chopped fresh parsley
- 1/4 cup chopped fresh basil
- 1/4 cup chopped fresh mint
- 1/2 cup diced cucumber
- 1/2 cup cherry tomatoes, halved
- 1/4 cup Kalamata olives, pitted and sliced
- 1/4 cup crumbled feta cheese (optional)
- 2 tablespoons extra virgin olive oil
- 2 tablespoons red wine vinegar
- 1 clove garlic, minced
- Salt and pepper to taste
- Optional: lemon wedges for serving

Instructions:

1. In a large mixing bowl, combine the drained and rinsed chickpeas, kidney beans, and cannellini beans.
2. Add the finely chopped red onion, chopped fresh parsley, chopped fresh basil, chopped fresh mint, diced cucumber, halved cherry tomatoes, sliced Kalamata olives, and crumbled feta cheese (if using) to the bowl with the mixed beans.
3. In a small bowl, whisk together the extra virgin olive oil, red wine vinegar, minced garlic, salt, and pepper to make the dressing.
4. Pour the dressing over the bean mixture in the large mixing bowl. Toss gently until everything is evenly coated with the dressing.
5. Taste and adjust seasoning if needed. You can add more salt, pepper, or vinegar according to your preference.
6. Chill the Mediterranean Three Bean Salad in the refrigerator for at least 30 minutes before serving to allow the flavors to meld together.
7. Serve the bean salad as a side dish or a light meal.

8. Optionally, serve with lemon wedges on the side for squeezing over the salad.
9. Enjoy your flavorful and nutritious Mediterranean Three Bean Salad!

Chicken and Farro Salad with Sun-Dried Tomatoes

Ingredients:

For the Chicken:

- 2 boneless, skinless chicken breasts
- 2 tablespoons olive oil
- 1 tablespoon lemon juice
- 2 cloves garlic, minced
- 1 teaspoon dried oregano
- Salt and pepper to taste

For the Salad:

- 1 cup farro
- 2 cups water or chicken broth
- 1/2 cup sun-dried tomatoes, chopped
- 1/2 cup chopped roasted red peppers
- 1/4 cup chopped fresh parsley
- 1/4 cup chopped fresh basil
- 1/4 cup crumbled feta cheese (optional)
- 2 tablespoons extra virgin olive oil
- 1 tablespoon balsamic vinegar
- Salt and pepper to taste

Instructions:

1. Preheat your grill to medium-high heat.
2. In a bowl, combine the olive oil, lemon juice, minced garlic, dried oregano, salt, and pepper. Place the chicken breasts in a shallow dish or a resealable plastic bag and pour the marinade over them. Make sure the chicken is evenly coated. Marinate in the refrigerator for at least 30 minutes, or up to 2 hours.
3. While the chicken is marinating, rinse the farro under cold water and drain it.
4. In a medium saucepan, bring the water or chicken broth to a boil. Add the farro and reduce the heat to low. Cover and simmer for 20-25 minutes, or until the farro is tender but still chewy. Drain any excess liquid and let the farro cool.

5. Once the grill is preheated, remove the chicken breasts from the marinade and discard any excess marinade. Grill the chicken breasts for 6-8 minutes per side, or until they are cooked through and no longer pink in the center. Remove from the grill and let them rest for a few minutes before slicing.
6. In a large mixing bowl, combine the cooked and cooled farro, chopped sun-dried tomatoes, chopped roasted red peppers, chopped fresh parsley, and chopped fresh basil. If using, add the crumbled feta cheese.
7. In a small bowl, whisk together the extra virgin olive oil and balsamic vinegar to make the dressing. Season with salt and pepper to taste.
8. Slice the grilled chicken breasts into thin strips.
9. Pour the dressing over the salad ingredients in the mixing bowl. Toss gently until everything is evenly coated with the dressing.
10. Divide the farro salad among serving plates or bowls.
11. Top each serving with the sliced grilled chicken.
12. Enjoy your flavorful and nutritious Chicken and Farro Salad with Sun-Dried Tomatoes!

Greek Pasta Salad with Chicken

Ingredients:

For the Chicken:

- 2 boneless, skinless chicken breasts
- 2 tablespoons olive oil
- 1 tablespoon lemon juice
- 2 cloves garlic, minced
- 1 teaspoon dried oregano
- Salt and pepper to taste

For the Pasta Salad:

- 8 ounces pasta (such as penne or rotini)
- 1 cup cherry tomatoes, halved
- 1 cucumber, diced
- 1/2 red onion, thinly sliced
- 1/2 cup Kalamata olives, pitted and sliced
- 1/2 cup crumbled feta cheese
- 1/4 cup chopped fresh parsley
- 2 tablespoons chopped fresh dill (optional)
- 2 tablespoons extra virgin olive oil
- 1 tablespoon red wine vinegar
- Salt and pepper to taste
- Optional: lemon wedges for serving

Instructions:

1. Preheat your grill to medium-high heat.
2. In a bowl, combine the olive oil, lemon juice, minced garlic, dried oregano, salt, and pepper. Place the chicken breasts in a shallow dish or a resealable plastic bag and pour the marinade over them. Make sure the chicken is evenly coated. Marinate in the refrigerator for at least 30 minutes, or up to 2 hours.
3. Cook the pasta according to the package instructions until al dente. Drain and rinse under cold water to stop the cooking process. Let it cool.

4. While the pasta is cooking, prepare the other salad ingredients. In a large mixing bowl, combine the halved cherry tomatoes, diced cucumber, thinly sliced red onion, sliced Kalamata olives, crumbled feta cheese, chopped fresh parsley, and chopped fresh dill (if using).
5. In a small bowl, whisk together the extra virgin olive oil and red wine vinegar to make the dressing. Season with salt and pepper to taste.
6. Once the grill is preheated, remove the chicken breasts from the marinade and discard any excess marinade. Grill the chicken breasts for 6-8 minutes per side, or until they are cooked through and no longer pink in the center. Remove from the grill and let them rest for a few minutes before slicing.
7. Add the cooled pasta to the mixing bowl with the other salad ingredients.
8. Pour the dressing over the pasta salad ingredients. Toss gently until everything is evenly coated with the dressing.
9. Slice the grilled chicken breasts into thin strips.
10. Serve the Greek Pasta Salad in individual bowls or plates, topping each serving with the sliced grilled chicken.
11. Optionally, serve with lemon wedges on the side for squeezing over the salad.
12. Enjoy your flavorful and nutritious Greek Pasta Salad with Chicken!

Quinoa and Black Bean Salad with Avocado

Ingredients:

- 1 cup quinoa
- 2 cups water or vegetable broth
- 1 can (15 ounces) black beans, drained and rinsed
- 1 avocado, diced
- 1 cup cherry tomatoes, halved
- 1/2 red onion, finely chopped
- 1/4 cup chopped fresh cilantro
- 1/4 cup chopped fresh parsley
- Juice of 1 lime
- 2 tablespoons extra virgin olive oil
- 1 clove garlic, minced
- Salt and pepper to taste
- Optional: diced jalapeño for heat

Instructions:

1. Rinse the quinoa under cold water using a fine-mesh sieve.
2. In a medium saucepan, combine the quinoa and water or vegetable broth. Bring to a boil over medium-high heat, then reduce the heat to low. Cover and simmer for 15-20 minutes, or until the quinoa is cooked and the liquid is absorbed. Remove from heat and let it cool.
3. In a large mixing bowl, combine the cooked quinoa, drained and rinsed black beans, diced avocado, halved cherry tomatoes, finely chopped red onion, chopped fresh cilantro, and chopped fresh parsley.
4. In a small bowl, whisk together the lime juice, extra virgin olive oil, minced garlic, salt, and pepper. If you want some heat, you can also add some diced jalapeño to the dressing.
5. Pour the dressing over the quinoa and black bean mixture in the large mixing bowl. Toss gently until everything is evenly coated with the dressing.
6. Taste and adjust seasoning if needed. Add more salt, pepper, or lime juice according to your preference.
7. Chill the Quinoa and Black Bean Salad in the refrigerator for at least 30 minutes before serving to allow the flavors to meld together.
8. Serve the salad as a side dish or a light meal.

9. Enjoy your nutritious and delicious Quinoa and Black Bean Salad with Avocado!

Grilled Lamb and Couscous Salad

Ingredients:

For the Grilled Lamb:

- 1 pound lamb loin chops or leg of lamb, trimmed of excess fat
- 2 tablespoons olive oil
- 2 cloves garlic, minced
- 1 teaspoon dried rosemary
- 1 teaspoon dried thyme
- Salt and pepper to taste

For the Couscous Salad:

- 1 cup couscous
- 1 1/4 cups vegetable broth or water
- 1 cucumber, diced
- 1 cup cherry tomatoes, halved
- 1/2 red onion, finely chopped
- 1/2 cup Kalamata olives, pitted and sliced
- 1/4 cup crumbled feta cheese
- 1/4 cup chopped fresh parsley
- 2 tablespoons chopped fresh mint
- 2 tablespoons extra virgin olive oil
- 2 tablespoons lemon juice
- Salt and pepper to taste

Instructions:

1. Preheat your grill to medium-high heat.
2. In a bowl, combine the olive oil, minced garlic, dried rosemary, dried thyme, salt, and pepper. Place the lamb chops in a shallow dish or a resealable plastic bag and pour the marinade over them. Make sure the lamb chops are evenly coated. Marinate in the refrigerator for at least 30 minutes, or up to 2 hours.

3. While the lamb is marinating, prepare the couscous. In a medium saucepan, bring the vegetable broth or water to a boil. Stir in the couscous, cover, and remove from heat. Let it sit for 5 minutes, then fluff it with a fork. Let it cool.
4. Once the grill is preheated, remove the lamb chops from the marinade and discard any excess marinade. Place the lamb chops on the grill and cook for 3-4 minutes per side for medium-rare, or longer to your desired level of doneness. Remove from the grill and let them rest for a few minutes before slicing.
5. In a large mixing bowl, combine the cooked and cooled couscous, diced cucumber, halved cherry tomatoes, finely chopped red onion, sliced Kalamata olives, crumbled feta cheese, chopped fresh parsley, and chopped fresh mint.
6. In a small bowl, whisk together the extra virgin olive oil and lemon juice to make the dressing. Season with salt and pepper to taste.
7. Pour the dressing over the couscous salad ingredients in the mixing bowl. Toss gently until everything is evenly coated with the dressing.
8. Taste and adjust seasoning if needed.
9. Serve the Grilled Lamb and Couscous Salad with the sliced grilled lamb chops on top.
10. Enjoy your flavorful and satisfying salad!

Mediterranean Eggplant and Chickpea Salad

Ingredients:

For the Eggplant and Chickpeas:

- 1 large eggplant, diced into small cubes
- 1 can (15 ounces) chickpeas, drained and rinsed
- 3 tablespoons olive oil
- 1 teaspoon paprika
- 1 teaspoon ground cumin
- 1/2 teaspoon garlic powder
- Salt and pepper to taste

For the Salad:

- 2 cups cherry tomatoes, halved
- 1/2 red onion, thinly sliced
- 1/2 cup Kalamata olives, pitted and sliced
- 1/4 cup chopped fresh parsley
- 1/4 cup chopped fresh mint
- 1/4 cup crumbled feta cheese
- Juice of 1 lemon
- 2 tablespoons extra virgin olive oil
- Salt and pepper to taste

Instructions:

1. Preheat your oven to 425°F (220°C).
2. In a large mixing bowl, combine the diced eggplant, drained and rinsed chickpeas, olive oil, paprika, ground cumin, garlic powder, salt, and pepper. Toss until the eggplant and chickpeas are evenly coated with the seasoning.
3. Spread the seasoned eggplant and chickpeas in a single layer on a baking sheet lined with parchment paper or aluminum foil.

4. Roast in the preheated oven for 25-30 minutes, or until the eggplant is tender and golden brown, stirring halfway through cooking.
5. While the eggplant and chickpeas are roasting, prepare the other salad ingredients. In a large salad bowl, combine the halved cherry tomatoes, thinly sliced red onion, sliced Kalamata olives, chopped fresh parsley, chopped fresh mint, and crumbled feta cheese.
6. In a small bowl, whisk together the lemon juice and extra virgin olive oil to make the dressing. Season with salt and pepper to taste.
7. Once the eggplant and chickpeas are done roasting, let them cool slightly.
8. Add the roasted eggplant and chickpeas to the salad bowl with the other ingredients.
9. Pour the dressing over the salad ingredients. Toss gently until everything is evenly coated with the dressing.
10. Taste and adjust seasoning if needed.
11. Serve the Mediterranean Eggplant and Chickpea Salad immediately, or chill it in the refrigerator for at least 30 minutes before serving to allow the flavors to meld together.
12. Enjoy your flavorful and nutritious salad!

Turkey and Bulgur Salad with Pistachios

Ingredients:

For the Turkey:

- 1 pound ground turkey
- 2 tablespoons olive oil
- 2 cloves garlic, minced
- 1 teaspoon ground cumin
- 1 teaspoon ground coriander
- 1/2 teaspoon paprika
- Salt and pepper to taste

For the Salad:

- 1 cup bulgur wheat
- 2 cups water or chicken broth
- 1/2 cup shelled pistachios, chopped
- 1/2 cup dried cranberries or raisins
- 1/4 cup chopped fresh parsley
- 1/4 cup chopped fresh mint
- 1/4 cup chopped green onions
- 1/4 cup crumbled feta cheese (optional)
- Juice of 1 lemon
- 2 tablespoons extra virgin olive oil
- Salt and pepper to taste

Instructions:

1. In a large skillet, heat the olive oil over medium heat. Add the minced garlic and cook for about 1 minute until fragrant.
2. Add the ground turkey to the skillet, breaking it apart with a spatula. Cook until the turkey is browned and cooked through, about 5-7 minutes.
3. Stir in the ground cumin, ground coriander, paprika, salt, and pepper. Cook for another 2-3 minutes, stirring occasionally, to allow the flavors to meld together. Remove from heat and set aside.

4. In a medium saucepan, bring the water or chicken broth to a boil. Add the bulgur wheat and reduce the heat to low. Cover and simmer for 10-12 minutes, or until the bulgur is tender and the liquid is absorbed. Remove from heat and let it cool.
5. In a large mixing bowl, combine the cooked bulgur wheat, chopped pistachios, dried cranberries or raisins, chopped fresh parsley, chopped fresh mint, chopped green onions, and crumbled feta cheese (if using).
6. In a small bowl, whisk together the lemon juice and extra virgin olive oil to make the dressing. Season with salt and pepper to taste.
7. Pour the dressing over the salad ingredients in the mixing bowl. Toss gently until everything is evenly coated with the dressing.
8. Add the cooked ground turkey to the salad bowl. Toss gently to combine.
9. Taste and adjust seasoning if needed.
10. Serve the Turkey and Bulgur Salad with Pistachios immediately, or chill it in the refrigerator for at least 30 minutes before serving to allow the flavors to meld together.
11. Enjoy your flavorful and nutritious salad!

Greek Yogurt Chicken Salad

Ingredients:

For the Chicken:

- 2 boneless, skinless chicken breasts
- 2 tablespoons olive oil
- 1 teaspoon dried oregano
- 1 teaspoon dried thyme
- Salt and pepper to taste

For the Salad:

- 1/2 cup Greek yogurt
- 1 tablespoon lemon juice
- 1 tablespoon Dijon mustard
- 1 clove garlic, minced
- 1/4 cup chopped fresh parsley
- 1/4 cup chopped fresh dill
- 1/4 cup chopped red onion
- 1/4 cup chopped celery
- 1/4 cup chopped cucumber
- 1/4 cup chopped red bell pepper
- Salt and pepper to taste

Instructions:

1. Preheat your grill to medium-high heat.
2. In a bowl, combine the olive oil, dried oregano, dried thyme, salt, and pepper. Place the chicken breasts in a shallow dish or a resealable plastic bag and pour the marinade over them. Make sure the chicken is evenly coated. Marinate in the refrigerator for at least 30 minutes, or up to 2 hours.
3. Once the grill is preheated, remove the chicken breasts from the marinade and discard any excess marinade. Grill the chicken breasts for 6-8 minutes per side,

or until they are cooked through and no longer pink in the center. Remove from the grill and let them rest for a few minutes before slicing.
4. While the chicken is grilling, prepare the salad dressing. In a small bowl, whisk together the Greek yogurt, lemon juice, Dijon mustard, minced garlic, chopped fresh parsley, and chopped fresh dill. Season with salt and pepper to taste.
5. In a large mixing bowl, combine the chopped red onion, chopped celery, chopped cucumber, and chopped red bell pepper.
6. Once the grilled chicken breasts have rested, slice them into bite-sized pieces.
7. Add the sliced grilled chicken to the mixing bowl with the vegetables.
8. Pour the Greek yogurt dressing over the chicken and vegetables in the mixing bowl. Toss gently until everything is evenly coated with the dressing.
9. Taste and adjust seasoning if needed.
10. Serve the Greek Yogurt Chicken Salad immediately, or chill it in the refrigerator for at least 30 minutes before serving to allow the flavors to meld together.
11. Enjoy your flavorful and protein-packed salad!

Lentil and Tuna Salad with Capers

Ingredients:

- 1 cup dried green or brown lentils
- 3 cups water or vegetable broth
- 2 cans (5 ounces each) tuna in water, drained
- 1/4 cup capers, drained and rinsed
- 1/4 cup chopped red onion
- 1/4 cup chopped fresh parsley
- 2 tablespoons chopped fresh dill
- 2 tablespoons extra virgin olive oil
- 2 tablespoons red wine vinegar
- Salt and pepper to taste
- Optional: lemon wedges for serving

Instructions:

1. Rinse the lentils under cold water in a fine-mesh sieve.
2. In a medium saucepan, combine the rinsed lentils and water or vegetable broth. Bring to a boil over medium-high heat, then reduce the heat to low. Cover and simmer for 20-25 minutes, or until the lentils are tender but still hold their shape. Drain any excess liquid and let the lentils cool.
3. In a large mixing bowl, flake the drained tuna with a fork.
4. Add the cooked and cooled lentils to the mixing bowl with the flaked tuna.
5. Add the drained and rinsed capers, chopped red onion, chopped fresh parsley, and chopped fresh dill to the mixing bowl.
6. In a small bowl, whisk together the extra virgin olive oil and red wine vinegar to make the dressing. Season with salt and pepper to taste.
7. Pour the dressing over the salad ingredients in the mixing bowl. Toss gently until everything is evenly coated with the dressing.
8. Taste and adjust seasoning if needed.
9. Serve the Lentil and Tuna Salad with Capers immediately, or chill it in the refrigerator for at least 30 minutes before serving to allow the flavors to meld together.
10. Optionally, serve with lemon wedges on the side for squeezing over the salad.
11. Enjoy your flavorful and protein-packed salad!

Mediterranean Cauliflower Salad with Tahini Dressing

Ingredients:

For the Cauliflower:

- 1 large head cauliflower, cut into florets
- 2 tablespoons olive oil
- 1 teaspoon ground cumin
- 1 teaspoon paprika
- Salt and pepper to taste

For the Salad:

- 1/2 cup cooked chickpeas (canned or cooked from dry)
- 1/4 cup chopped roasted red peppers
- 1/4 cup pitted Kalamata olives, halved
- 2 tablespoons chopped fresh parsley
- 2 tablespoons chopped fresh mint
- 2 tablespoons chopped fresh cilantro
- Optional: crumbled feta cheese for serving

For the Tahini Dressing:

- 1/4 cup tahini
- 2 tablespoons lemon juice
- 2 tablespoons water
- 1 clove garlic, minced
- Salt and pepper to taste

Instructions:

1. Preheat your oven to 425°F (220°C).

2. In a large mixing bowl, toss the cauliflower florets with olive oil, ground cumin, paprika, salt, and pepper until evenly coated.
3. Spread the seasoned cauliflower florets in a single layer on a baking sheet lined with parchment paper or aluminum foil.
4. Roast the cauliflower in the preheated oven for 25-30 minutes, or until tender and golden brown, stirring halfway through cooking.
5. While the cauliflower is roasting, prepare the other salad ingredients. In a large salad bowl, combine the cooked chickpeas, chopped roasted red peppers, halved Kalamata olives, chopped fresh parsley, chopped fresh mint, and chopped fresh cilantro.
6. In a small bowl, whisk together the tahini, lemon juice, water, minced garlic, salt, and pepper to make the dressing. If the dressing is too thick, add more water, 1 tablespoon at a time, until desired consistency is reached.
7. Once the cauliflower is done roasting, let it cool slightly.
8. Add the roasted cauliflower to the salad bowl with the other ingredients.
9. Pour the tahini dressing over the salad ingredients. Toss gently until everything is evenly coated with the dressing.
10. Taste and adjust seasoning if needed.
11. Optionally, sprinkle crumbled feta cheese over the salad before serving.
12. Serve the Mediterranean Cauliflower Salad immediately, or chill it in the refrigerator for at least 30 minutes before serving to allow the flavors to meld together.
13. Enjoy your flavorful and nutritious salad!

Grilled Swordfish and White Bean Salad

Ingredients:

For the Swordfish:

- 2 swordfish steaks
- 2 tablespoons olive oil
- 1 tablespoon lemon juice
- 2 cloves garlic, minced
- 1 teaspoon dried oregano
- Salt and pepper to taste

For the White Bean Salad:

- 2 cans (15 ounces each) white beans (such as cannellini or navy), drained and rinsed
- 1/2 red onion, finely chopped
- 1 cup cherry tomatoes, halved
- 1/4 cup chopped fresh parsley
- 2 tablespoons chopped fresh basil
- 2 tablespoons chopped fresh mint
- 1/4 cup Kalamata olives, pitted and sliced
- 2 tablespoons extra virgin olive oil
- 2 tablespoons red wine vinegar
- Salt and pepper to taste

Instructions:

1. Preheat your grill to medium-high heat.
2. In a bowl, combine the olive oil, lemon juice, minced garlic, dried oregano, salt, and pepper. Place the swordfish steaks in a shallow dish or a resealable plastic bag and pour the marinade over them. Make sure the swordfish steaks are evenly coated. Marinate in the refrigerator for at least 30 minutes, or up to 2 hours.
3. While the swordfish is marinating, prepare the white bean salad. In a large mixing bowl, combine the drained and rinsed white beans, finely chopped red onion,

halved cherry tomatoes, chopped fresh parsley, chopped fresh basil, chopped fresh mint, and sliced Kalamata olives.
4. In a small bowl, whisk together the extra virgin olive oil and red wine vinegar to make the dressing. Season with salt and pepper to taste.
5. Pour the dressing over the white bean salad ingredients in the mixing bowl. Toss gently until everything is evenly coated with the dressing.
6. Once the grill is preheated, remove the swordfish steaks from the marinade and discard any excess marinade. Place the swordfish steaks on the grill and cook for 4-5 minutes per side, or until they are cooked through and opaque in the center. Remove from the grill and let them rest for a few minutes.
7. Divide the white bean salad among serving plates or bowls.
8. Place a grilled swordfish steak on top of each serving of the white bean salad.
9. Serve the Grilled Swordfish and White Bean Salad immediately.
10. Enjoy your flavorful and protein-packed meal!

Greek Spinach Salad with Grilled Halloumi

Ingredients:

For the Grilled Halloumi:

- 1 block (about 8 ounces) halloumi cheese, sliced into 1/4 inch thick slices
- 1 tablespoon olive oil

For the Salad:

- 8 cups fresh spinach leaves, washed and dried
- 1 cup cherry tomatoes, halved
- 1/2 English cucumber, sliced
- 1/4 cup Kalamata olives, pitted
- 1/4 cup thinly sliced red onion
- 1/4 cup crumbled feta cheese
- 2 tablespoons chopped fresh dill
- 2 tablespoons chopped fresh parsley

For the Dressing:

- 3 tablespoons extra virgin olive oil
- 2 tablespoons red wine vinegar
- 1 tablespoon lemon juice
- 1 clove garlic, minced
- 1 teaspoon dried oregano
- Salt and pepper to taste

Instructions:

1. Preheat your grill or grill pan over medium-high heat.
2. Brush the halloumi slices on both sides with olive oil.

3. Grill the halloumi slices for about 2-3 minutes on each side, or until grill marks appear and the cheese is softened and slightly golden. Remove from the grill and set aside.
4. In a large salad bowl, combine the fresh spinach leaves, halved cherry tomatoes, sliced cucumber, Kalamata olives, thinly sliced red onion, crumbled feta cheese, chopped fresh dill, and chopped fresh parsley.
5. In a small bowl, whisk together the extra virgin olive oil, red wine vinegar, lemon juice, minced garlic, dried oregano, salt, and pepper to make the dressing.
6. Pour the dressing over the salad ingredients in the bowl. Toss gently until everything is evenly coated with the dressing.
7. Divide the Greek spinach salad among serving plates.
8. Arrange the grilled halloumi slices on top of each serving of the salad.
9. Serve the Greek Spinach Salad with Grilled Halloumi immediately.
10. Enjoy your delicious and nutritious salad!

Quinoa and Edamame Salad with Lemon Vinaigrette

Ingredients:

For the Salad:

- 1 cup quinoa
- 2 cups water or vegetable broth
- 1 cup shelled edamame, cooked according to package instructions
- 1 red bell pepper, diced
- 1/2 English cucumber, diced
- 1/4 cup chopped red onion
- 1/4 cup chopped fresh cilantro or parsley
- 1/4 cup chopped fresh mint
- 1/4 cup crumbled feta cheese (optional)
- Salt and pepper to taste

For the Lemon Vinaigrette:

- 1/4 cup extra virgin olive oil
- 2 tablespoons fresh lemon juice
- 1 teaspoon lemon zest
- 1 clove garlic, minced
- 1 teaspoon Dijon mustard
- Salt and pepper to taste

Instructions:

1. Rinse the quinoa under cold water in a fine-mesh sieve.
2. In a medium saucepan, bring the water or vegetable broth to a boil. Stir in the quinoa, cover, and reduce the heat to low. Simmer for 15-20 minutes, or until the quinoa is cooked and the liquid is absorbed. Remove from heat and let it cool.
3. In a large mixing bowl, combine the cooked and cooled quinoa, cooked edamame, diced red bell pepper, diced cucumber, chopped red onion, chopped fresh cilantro or parsley, chopped fresh mint, and crumbled feta cheese (if using).

4. In a small bowl, whisk together the extra virgin olive oil, fresh lemon juice, lemon zest, minced garlic, Dijon mustard, salt, and pepper to make the lemon vinaigrette.
5. Pour the lemon vinaigrette over the salad ingredients in the mixing bowl. Toss gently until everything is evenly coated with the dressing.
6. Taste and adjust seasoning if needed.
7. Serve the Quinoa and Edamame Salad with Lemon Vinaigrette immediately, or chill it in the refrigerator for at least 30 minutes before serving to allow the flavors to meld together.
8. Enjoy your flavorful and nutritious salad!

Mediterranean Zucchini Ribbon Salad with Pine Nuts

Ingredients:

For the Salad:

- 4 medium zucchini
- 1/4 cup pine nuts, toasted
- 1/4 cup crumbled feta cheese
- 1/4 cup Kalamata olives, pitted and halved
- 2 tablespoons chopped fresh basil
- 2 tablespoons chopped fresh mint
- Salt and pepper to taste

For the Dressing:

- 3 tablespoons extra virgin olive oil
- 2 tablespoons lemon juice
- 1 clove garlic, minced
- 1 teaspoon Dijon mustard
- Salt and pepper to taste

Instructions:

1. Using a vegetable peeler or a mandoline slicer, slice the zucchini lengthwise into thin ribbons. Place the ribbons in a large mixing bowl.
2. In a small skillet over medium heat, toast the pine nuts until golden brown and fragrant, stirring frequently to prevent burning. Remove from heat and set aside.
3. Add the toasted pine nuts, crumbled feta cheese, halved Kalamata olives, chopped fresh basil, and chopped fresh mint to the mixing bowl with the zucchini ribbons.
4. In a small bowl, whisk together the extra virgin olive oil, lemon juice, minced garlic, Dijon mustard, salt, and pepper to make the dressing.
5. Pour the dressing over the salad ingredients in the mixing bowl. Toss gently until everything is evenly coated with the dressing.

6. Taste and adjust seasoning if needed.
7. Serve the Mediterranean Zucchini Ribbon Salad with Pine Nuts immediately, or chill it in the refrigerator for at least 30 minutes before serving to allow the flavors to meld together.
8. Enjoy your refreshing and flavorful salad!

Chicken and White Bean Salad with Pesto

Ingredients:

For the Chicken:

- 2 boneless, skinless chicken breasts
- 2 tablespoons olive oil
- 2 cloves garlic, minced
- 1 teaspoon dried basil
- 1 teaspoon dried oregano
- Salt and pepper to taste

For the Salad:

- 1 can (15 ounces) white beans (such as cannellini or navy), drained and rinsed
- 1 cup cherry tomatoes, halved
- 1/2 English cucumber, diced
- 1/4 cup sliced red onion
- 1/4 cup chopped fresh parsley
- 1/4 cup chopped fresh basil
- 1/4 cup pine nuts, toasted
- Salt and pepper to taste

For the Pesto:

- 2 cups fresh basil leaves
- 1/4 cup pine nuts, toasted
- 1/4 cup grated Parmesan cheese
- 2 cloves garlic, minced
- 1/4 cup extra virgin olive oil
- Salt and pepper to taste

Instructions:

1. Preheat your grill or grill pan over medium-high heat.

2. In a bowl, combine the olive oil, minced garlic, dried basil, dried oregano, salt, and pepper. Place the chicken breasts in a shallow dish or a resealable plastic bag and pour the marinade over them. Make sure the chicken breasts are evenly coated. Marinate in the refrigerator for at least 30 minutes, or up to 2 hours.
3. While the chicken is marinating, prepare the pesto. In a food processor, combine the fresh basil leaves, toasted pine nuts, grated Parmesan cheese, minced garlic, extra virgin olive oil, salt, and pepper. Blend until smooth, scraping down the sides as needed. Adjust seasoning to taste.
4. Grill the marinated chicken breasts for 6-8 minutes per side, or until they are cooked through and no longer pink in the center. Remove from the grill and let them rest for a few minutes before slicing.
5. In a large mixing bowl, combine the drained and rinsed white beans, halved cherry tomatoes, diced cucumber, sliced red onion, chopped fresh parsley, chopped fresh basil, and toasted pine nuts.
6. Add the sliced grilled chicken to the salad bowl.
7. Pour the prepared pesto over the salad ingredients in the mixing bowl. Toss gently until everything is evenly coated with the pesto.
8. Taste and adjust seasoning if needed.
9. Serve the Chicken and White Bean Salad with Pesto immediately.
10. Enjoy your flavorful and protein-packed salad!

Greek Kale Salad with Quinoa and Cranberries

Ingredients:

For the Salad:

- 1 bunch kale, stems removed and leaves thinly sliced
- 1 cup cooked quinoa, cooled
- 1/2 cup dried cranberries
- 1/2 cup crumbled feta cheese
- 1/4 cup chopped red onion
- 1/4 cup chopped fresh parsley
- 1/4 cup chopped fresh dill
- 1/4 cup chopped fresh mint
- 1/4 cup chopped Kalamata olives
- Optional: 1/4 cup chopped toasted walnuts or almonds

For the Dressing:

- 1/4 cup extra virgin olive oil
- 2 tablespoons red wine vinegar
- 1 tablespoon lemon juice
- 1 teaspoon Dijon mustard
- 1 clove garlic, minced
- Salt and pepper to taste

Instructions:

1. In a large mixing bowl, combine the thinly sliced kale leaves, cooked and cooled quinoa, dried cranberries, crumbled feta cheese, chopped red onion, chopped fresh parsley, chopped fresh dill, chopped fresh mint, and chopped Kalamata olives. If using, add the chopped toasted walnuts or almonds.
2. In a small bowl, whisk together the extra virgin olive oil, red wine vinegar, lemon juice, Dijon mustard, minced garlic, salt, and pepper to make the dressing.

3. Pour the dressing over the salad ingredients in the mixing bowl. Toss gently until everything is evenly coated with the dressing.
4. Taste and adjust seasoning if needed.
5. Serve the Greek Kale Salad with Quinoa and Cranberries immediately, or chill it in the refrigerator for at least 30 minutes before serving to allow the flavors to meld together.
6. Enjoy your flavorful and nutritious salad!

Lentil and Chicken Salad with Yogurt Dressing

Ingredients:

For the Salad:

- 1 cup dried green or brown lentils
- 2 cups water or vegetable broth
- 2 boneless, skinless chicken breasts
- 2 tablespoons olive oil
- 1 teaspoon dried thyme
- 1 teaspoon dried rosemary
- Salt and pepper to taste
- 1 cup cherry tomatoes, halved
- 1 cucumber, diced
- 1/4 cup chopped red onion
- 1/4 cup chopped fresh parsley
- 1/4 cup crumbled feta cheese (optional)

For the Yogurt Dressing:

- 1/2 cup Greek yogurt
- 2 tablespoons lemon juice
- 1 tablespoon extra virgin olive oil
- 1 clove garlic, minced
- 1 teaspoon dried oregano
- Salt and pepper to taste

Instructions:

1. Rinse the lentils under cold water in a fine-mesh sieve.
2. In a medium saucepan, bring the water or vegetable broth to a boil. Stir in the lentils, cover, and reduce the heat to low. Simmer for 20-25 minutes, or until the lentils are tender but still hold their shape. Drain any excess liquid and let the lentils cool.
3. Preheat your grill or grill pan over medium-high heat.

4. In a bowl, combine the olive oil, dried thyme, dried rosemary, salt, and pepper. Place the chicken breasts in a shallow dish or a resealable plastic bag and pour the marinade over them. Make sure the chicken breasts are evenly coated. Marinate for at least 30 minutes.
5. Grill the chicken breasts for 6-8 minutes per side, or until they are cooked through and no longer pink in the center. Remove from the grill and let them rest for a few minutes before slicing.
6. In a large mixing bowl, combine the cooked and cooled lentils, halved cherry tomatoes, diced cucumber, chopped red onion, chopped fresh parsley, and crumbled feta cheese (if using).
7. In a small bowl, whisk together the Greek yogurt, lemon juice, extra virgin olive oil, minced garlic, dried oregano, salt, and pepper to make the dressing.
8. Pour the yogurt dressing over the salad ingredients in the mixing bowl. Toss gently until everything is evenly coated with the dressing.
9. Divide the lentil and chicken salad among serving plates.
10. Top each serving with sliced grilled chicken.
11. Serve the Lentil and Chicken Salad with Yogurt Dressing immediately.
12. Enjoy your flavorful and protein-packed salad!

Mediterranean Chickpea and Tomato Salad

Ingredients:

- 2 cans (15 ounces each) chickpeas, drained and rinsed
- 2 cups cherry tomatoes, halved
- 1/2 English cucumber, diced
- 1/4 cup sliced red onion
- 1/4 cup chopped fresh parsley
- 1/4 cup chopped fresh mint
- 1/4 cup chopped Kalamata olives
- 1/4 cup crumbled feta cheese (optional)
- Salt and pepper to taste

For the Dressing:

- 1/4 cup extra virgin olive oil
- 2 tablespoons red wine vinegar
- 1 clove garlic, minced
- 1 teaspoon dried oregano
- Salt and pepper to taste

Instructions:

1. In a large mixing bowl, combine the drained and rinsed chickpeas, halved cherry tomatoes, diced cucumber, sliced red onion, chopped fresh parsley, chopped fresh mint, chopped Kalamata olives, and crumbled feta cheese (if using).
2. In a small bowl, whisk together the extra virgin olive oil, red wine vinegar, minced garlic, dried oregano, salt, and pepper to make the dressing.
3. Pour the dressing over the salad ingredients in the mixing bowl. Toss gently until everything is evenly coated with the dressing.
4. Taste and adjust seasoning if needed.
5. Serve the Mediterranean Chickpea and Tomato Salad immediately, or chill it in the refrigerator for at least 30 minutes before serving to allow the flavors to meld together.
6. Enjoy your refreshing and flavorful salad!

Grilled Turkey and Vegetable Salad with Feta

Ingredients:

For the Grilled Turkey:

- 1 pound turkey breast cutlets
- 2 tablespoons olive oil
- 1 teaspoon dried oregano
- 1 teaspoon dried thyme
- Salt and pepper to taste

For the Salad:

- 4 cups mixed salad greens (such as romaine, spinach, or arugula)
- 1 red bell pepper, sliced
- 1 yellow bell pepper, sliced
- 1 zucchini, sliced
- 1 yellow squash, sliced
- 1 red onion, sliced
- 1/4 cup crumbled feta cheese
- 2 tablespoons chopped fresh parsley
- 2 tablespoons chopped fresh basil

For the Dressing:

- 1/4 cup extra virgin olive oil
- 2 tablespoons red wine vinegar
- 1 clove garlic, minced
- 1 teaspoon Dijon mustard
- Salt and pepper to taste

Instructions:

1. Preheat your grill or grill pan over medium-high heat.
2. In a bowl, combine the olive oil, dried oregano, dried thyme, salt, and pepper. Place the turkey breast cutlets in a shallow dish or a resealable plastic bag and pour the marinade over them. Make sure the turkey cutlets are evenly coated. Marinate for at least 30 minutes.
3. Grill the turkey breast cutlets for 3-4 minutes per side, or until they are cooked through and no longer pink in the center. Remove from the grill and let them rest for a few minutes before slicing.
4. While the turkey is grilling, prepare the vegetables. Place the sliced red bell pepper, yellow bell pepper, zucchini, yellow squash, and red onion on the grill. Grill for 3-4 minutes per side, or until they are tender and slightly charred. Remove from the grill and let them cool slightly.
5. In a large mixing bowl, combine the mixed salad greens, grilled vegetables, sliced grilled turkey breast cutlets, crumbled feta cheese, chopped fresh parsley, and chopped fresh basil.
6. In a small bowl, whisk together the extra virgin olive oil, red wine vinegar, minced garlic, Dijon mustard, salt, and pepper to make the dressing.
7. Pour the dressing over the salad ingredients in the mixing bowl. Toss gently until everything is evenly coated with the dressing.
8. Taste and adjust seasoning if needed.
9. Serve the Grilled Turkey and Vegetable Salad with Feta immediately.
10. Enjoy your flavorful and nutritious salad!

Greek-style Salmon Salad with Orzo

Ingredients:

For the Salmon:

- 4 salmon fillets (about 6 ounces each)
- 2 tablespoons olive oil
- 2 cloves garlic, minced
- 1 teaspoon dried oregano
- 1 teaspoon dried thyme
- Salt and pepper to taste

For the Salad:

- 1 cup orzo pasta
- 2 cups baby spinach leaves
- 1 cup cherry tomatoes, halved
- 1/2 English cucumber, diced
- 1/4 cup sliced red onion
- 1/4 cup pitted Kalamata olives, halved
- 1/4 cup crumbled feta cheese
- 2 tablespoons chopped fresh parsley
- 2 tablespoons chopped fresh dill

For the Dressing:

- 1/4 cup extra virgin olive oil
- 2 tablespoons red wine vinegar
- 1 clove garlic, minced
- 1 teaspoon Dijon mustard
- Salt and pepper to taste

Instructions:

1. Preheat your oven to 400°F (200°C).

2. In a small bowl, combine the olive oil, minced garlic, dried oregano, dried thyme, salt, and pepper. Place the salmon fillets in a shallow dish or a resealable plastic bag and pour the marinade over them. Make sure the salmon fillets are evenly coated. Marinate for about 15-20 minutes.
3. While the salmon is marinating, cook the orzo pasta according to the package instructions. Drain and set aside to cool.
4. Place the marinated salmon fillets on a baking sheet lined with parchment paper or aluminum foil. Bake in the preheated oven for 12-15 minutes, or until the salmon is cooked through and flakes easily with a fork. Remove from the oven and let them cool slightly.
5. In a large mixing bowl, combine the cooked and cooled orzo pasta, baby spinach leaves, halved cherry tomatoes, diced cucumber, sliced red onion, halved Kalamata olives, crumbled feta cheese, chopped fresh parsley, and chopped fresh dill.
6. In a small bowl, whisk together the extra virgin olive oil, red wine vinegar, minced garlic, Dijon mustard, salt, and pepper to make the dressing.
7. Pour the dressing over the salad ingredients in the mixing bowl. Toss gently until everything is evenly coated with the dressing.
8. Divide the salad among serving plates.
9. Top each serving with a baked salmon fillet.
10. Serve the Greek-style Salmon Salad with Orzo immediately.
11. Enjoy your flavorful and nutritious salad!

Quinoa and Roasted Vegetable Salad with Balsamic Glaze

Ingredients:

For the Salad:

- 1 cup quinoa
- 2 cups water or vegetable broth
- 2 cups mixed vegetables (such as bell peppers, zucchini, eggplant, cherry tomatoes)
- 2 tablespoons olive oil
- Salt and pepper to taste
- 1/4 cup crumbled feta cheese (optional)
- 2 tablespoons chopped fresh basil or parsley

For the Balsamic Glaze:

- 1/2 cup balsamic vinegar
- 1 tablespoon honey or maple syrup (optional)
- Salt and pepper to taste

Instructions:

1. Preheat your oven to 400°F (200°C).
2. Rinse the quinoa under cold water in a fine-mesh sieve.
3. In a medium saucepan, bring the water or vegetable broth to a boil. Stir in the quinoa, cover, and reduce the heat to low. Simmer for 15-20 minutes, or until the quinoa is cooked and the liquid is absorbed. Remove from heat and let it cool.
4. While the quinoa is cooking, prepare the vegetables. Chop the mixed vegetables into bite-sized pieces and place them on a baking sheet lined with parchment paper or aluminum foil. Drizzle with olive oil and season with salt and pepper to taste. Toss to coat evenly.
5. Roast the vegetables in the preheated oven for 20-25 minutes, or until they are tender and slightly caramelized, stirring halfway through cooking. Remove from the oven and let them cool slightly.

6. In a small saucepan, combine the balsamic vinegar and honey or maple syrup (if using) over medium heat. Bring to a simmer and cook for 10-15 minutes, or until the mixture is reduced by half and has thickened to a syrupy consistency. Remove from heat and let it cool.
7. In a large mixing bowl, combine the cooked and cooled quinoa, roasted vegetables, crumbled feta cheese (if using), and chopped fresh basil or parsley.
8. Drizzle the balsamic glaze over the salad ingredients in the mixing bowl. Toss gently until everything is evenly coated with the glaze.
9. Taste and adjust seasoning if needed.
10. Serve the Quinoa and Roasted Vegetable Salad with Balsamic Glaze immediately, or chill it in the refrigerator for at least 30 minutes before serving to allow the flavors to meld together.
11. Enjoy your flavorful and nutritious salad!

Mediterranean Bean Salad with Tuna

Ingredients:

- 2 cans (15 ounces each) mixed beans (such as cannellini beans, chickpeas, and kidney beans), drained and rinsed
- 2 cans (5 ounces each) tuna in water, drained
- 1 cup cherry tomatoes, halved
- 1/2 English cucumber, diced
- 1/4 cup sliced red onion
- 1/4 cup chopped fresh parsley
- 1/4 cup chopped fresh basil
- 1/4 cup pitted Kalamata olives, halved
- Salt and pepper to taste

For the Dressing:

- 1/4 cup extra virgin olive oil
- 2 tablespoons red wine vinegar
- 1 clove garlic, minced
- 1 teaspoon Dijon mustard
- 1 teaspoon dried oregano
- Salt and pepper to taste

Instructions:

1. In a large mixing bowl, combine the drained and rinsed mixed beans, drained tuna, halved cherry tomatoes, diced cucumber, sliced red onion, chopped fresh parsley, chopped fresh basil, and halved Kalamata olives.
2. In a small bowl, whisk together the extra virgin olive oil, red wine vinegar, minced garlic, Dijon mustard, dried oregano, salt, and pepper to make the dressing.
3. Pour the dressing over the salad ingredients in the mixing bowl. Toss gently until everything is evenly coated with the dressing.
4. Taste and adjust seasoning if needed.
5. Serve the Mediterranean Bean Salad with Tuna immediately, or chill it in the refrigerator for at least 30 minutes before serving to allow the flavors to meld together.

6. Enjoy your flavorful and protein-packed salad!

Greek Lentil Salad with Feta

Ingredients:

For the Salad:

- 1 cup dried green lentils
- 3 cups water
- 1 cucumber, diced
- 1 red bell pepper, diced
- 1/2 red onion, finely chopped
- 1 cup cherry tomatoes, halved
- 1/4 cup Kalamata olives, pitted and halved
- 1/4 cup crumbled feta cheese
- 2 tablespoons chopped fresh parsley
- 2 tablespoons chopped fresh dill

For the Dressing:

- 1/4 cup extra virgin olive oil
- 2 tablespoons red wine vinegar
- 1 clove garlic, minced
- 1 teaspoon dried oregano
- Salt and pepper to taste

Instructions:

1. Rinse the lentils under cold water in a fine-mesh sieve.
2. In a medium saucepan, bring the water to a boil. Add the lentils and reduce the heat to low. Simmer, uncovered, for 15-20 minutes, or until the lentils are tender but still hold their shape. Drain any excess water and let the lentils cool.
3. In a large mixing bowl, combine the cooked and cooled lentils, diced cucumber, diced red bell pepper, finely chopped red onion, halved cherry tomatoes, halved Kalamata olives, crumbled feta cheese, chopped fresh parsley, and chopped fresh dill.

4. In a small bowl, whisk together the extra virgin olive oil, red wine vinegar, minced garlic, dried oregano, salt, and pepper to make the dressing.
5. Pour the dressing over the salad ingredients in the mixing bowl. Toss gently until everything is evenly coated with the dressing.
6. Taste and adjust seasoning if needed.
7. Serve the Greek Lentil Salad with Feta immediately, or chill it in the refrigerator for at least 30 minutes before serving to allow the flavors to meld together.
8. Enjoy your flavorful and nutritious salad!

Grilled Chicken and Eggplant Salad

Ingredients:

For the Grilled Chicken:

- 2 boneless, skinless chicken breasts
- 2 tablespoons olive oil
- 2 cloves garlic, minced
- 1 teaspoon dried oregano
- Salt and pepper to taste

For the Grilled Eggplant:

- 1 large eggplant, sliced into rounds
- 2 tablespoons olive oil
- Salt and pepper to taste

For the Salad:

- 4 cups mixed salad greens (such as spinach, arugula, or romaine)
- 1 cup cherry tomatoes, halved
- 1/2 cucumber, sliced
- 1/4 cup red onion, thinly sliced
- 1/4 cup crumbled feta cheese
- 2 tablespoons chopped fresh parsley
- 2 tablespoons chopped fresh mint

For the Dressing:

- 1/4 cup extra virgin olive oil
- 2 tablespoons red wine vinegar
- 1 clove garlic, minced
- 1 teaspoon Dijon mustard

- Salt and pepper to taste

Instructions:

1. Preheat your grill or grill pan over medium-high heat.
2. In a bowl, combine the olive oil, minced garlic, dried oregano, salt, and pepper. Place the chicken breasts in a shallow dish or a resealable plastic bag and pour the marinade over them. Make sure the chicken breasts are evenly coated. Marinate for at least 30 minutes.
3. In a separate bowl, toss the sliced eggplant with olive oil, salt, and pepper until evenly coated.
4. Grill the chicken breasts for 6-8 minutes per side, or until they are cooked through and no longer pink in the center. Remove from the grill and let them rest for a few minutes before slicing.
5. Grill the sliced eggplant for 3-4 minutes per side, or until they are tender and have grill marks. Remove from the grill and let them cool slightly.
6. In a large mixing bowl, combine the mixed salad greens, halved cherry tomatoes, sliced cucumber, thinly sliced red onion, crumbled feta cheese, chopped fresh parsley, and chopped fresh mint.
7. In a small bowl, whisk together the extra virgin olive oil, red wine vinegar, minced garlic, Dijon mustard, salt, and pepper to make the dressing.
8. Pour the dressing over the salad ingredients in the mixing bowl. Toss gently until everything is evenly coated with the dressing.
9. Divide the salad among serving plates.
10. Top each serving with sliced grilled chicken and grilled eggplant.
11. Serve the Grilled Chicken and Eggplant Salad immediately.
12. Enjoy your flavorful and nutritious salad!

Mediterranean Bulgur Salad with Grilled Shrimp

Ingredients:

For the Grilled Shrimp:

- 1 pound large shrimp, peeled and deveined
- 2 tablespoons olive oil
- 2 cloves garlic, minced
- 1 teaspoon dried oregano
- Salt and pepper to taste
- Lemon wedges, for serving

For the Bulgur Salad:

- 1 cup bulgur wheat
- 1 1/2 cups boiling water or vegetable broth
- 1 cup cherry tomatoes, halved
- 1/2 English cucumber, diced
- 1/4 cup chopped red onion
- 1/4 cup pitted Kalamata olives, halved
- 1/4 cup crumbled feta cheese
- 2 tablespoons chopped fresh parsley
- 2 tablespoons chopped fresh mint

For the Dressing:

- 1/4 cup extra virgin olive oil
- 2 tablespoons red wine vinegar
- 1 clove garlic, minced
- 1 teaspoon Dijon mustard
- Salt and pepper to taste

Instructions:

1. In a bowl, combine the olive oil, minced garlic, dried oregano, salt, and pepper. Add the peeled and deveined shrimp to the bowl and toss until evenly coated. Let the shrimp marinate for about 15-30 minutes.
2. Meanwhile, prepare the bulgur wheat. Place the bulgur wheat in a heatproof bowl and pour the boiling water or vegetable broth over it. Cover the bowl with a lid or plate and let it sit for about 15-20 minutes, or until the bulgur is tender and has absorbed all the liquid. Fluff the bulgur with a fork and let it cool.
3. Preheat your grill or grill pan over medium-high heat. Thread the marinated shrimp onto skewers.
4. Grill the shrimp skewers for 2-3 minutes per side, or until they are pink and opaque. Remove from the grill and set aside.
5. In a large mixing bowl, combine the cooked and cooled bulgur wheat, halved cherry tomatoes, diced cucumber, chopped red onion, halved Kalamata olives, crumbled feta cheese, chopped fresh parsley, and chopped fresh mint.
6. In a small bowl, whisk together the extra virgin olive oil, red wine vinegar, minced garlic, Dijon mustard, salt, and pepper to make the dressing.
7. Pour the dressing over the salad ingredients in the mixing bowl. Toss gently until everything is evenly coated with the dressing.
8. Divide the bulgur salad among serving plates.
9. Top each serving with grilled shrimp skewers.
10. Serve the Mediterranean Bulgur Salad with Grilled Shrimp immediately, with lemon wedges on the side.
11. Enjoy your flavorful and protein-packed salad!

Greek-style Beef and Olive Salad

Ingredients:

For the Beef:

- 1 pound beef sirloin or flank steak, thinly sliced
- 2 tablespoons olive oil
- 2 cloves garlic, minced
- 1 teaspoon dried oregano
- Salt and pepper to taste

For the Salad:

- 4 cups mixed salad greens (such as romaine, spinach, or arugula)
- 1 cucumber, sliced
- 1 cup cherry tomatoes, halved
- 1/4 cup red onion, thinly sliced
- 1/4 cup pitted Kalamata olives
- 1/4 cup crumbled feta cheese

For the Dressing:

- 1/4 cup extra virgin olive oil
- 2 tablespoons red wine vinegar
- 1 clove garlic, minced
- 1 teaspoon Dijon mustard
- 1 teaspoon dried oregano
- Salt and pepper to taste

Instructions:

1. In a bowl, combine the olive oil, minced garlic, dried oregano, salt, and pepper. Add the thinly sliced beef to the bowl and toss until evenly coated. Let the beef marinate for about 15-30 minutes.
2. Heat a skillet or grill pan over medium-high heat. Cook the marinated beef slices for 2-3 minutes per side, or until they are cooked to your desired doneness. Remove from heat and let them rest for a few minutes.
3. In a large mixing bowl, combine the mixed salad greens, sliced cucumber, halved cherry tomatoes, thinly sliced red onion, pitted Kalamata olives, and crumbled feta cheese.
4. In a small bowl, whisk together the extra virgin olive oil, red wine vinegar, minced garlic, Dijon mustard, dried oregano, salt, and pepper to make the dressing.
5. Pour the dressing over the salad ingredients in the mixing bowl. Toss gently until everything is evenly coated with the dressing.
6. Divide the salad among serving plates.
7. Top each serving with the cooked beef slices.
8. Serve the Greek-style Beef and Olive Salad immediately.
9. Enjoy your flavorful and protein-packed salad!

Quinoa and Avocado Salad with Lemon-Tahini Dressing

Ingredients:

For the Salad:

- 1 cup quinoa, rinsed
- 2 cups water or vegetable broth
- 2 ripe avocados, diced
- 1 cup cherry tomatoes, halved
- 1/4 cup red onion, finely chopped
- 1/4 cup fresh cilantro, chopped
- 1/4 cup roasted pumpkin seeds (pepitas)
- Salt and pepper to taste

For the Lemon-Tahini Dressing:

- 1/4 cup tahini
- 2 tablespoons fresh lemon juice
- 2 tablespoons water
- 1 tablespoon extra virgin olive oil
- 1 clove garlic, minced
- 1 teaspoon honey or maple syrup (optional)
- Salt and pepper to taste

Instructions:

1. In a medium saucepan, bring the water or vegetable broth to a boil. Stir in the quinoa, cover, and reduce the heat to low. Simmer for 15-20 minutes, or until the quinoa is cooked and the liquid is absorbed. Remove from heat and let it cool.
2. In a large mixing bowl, combine the cooked and cooled quinoa, diced avocados, halved cherry tomatoes, finely chopped red onion, chopped fresh cilantro, and roasted pumpkin seeds.

3. In a small bowl, whisk together the tahini, fresh lemon juice, water, extra virgin olive oil, minced garlic, honey or maple syrup (if using), salt, and pepper to make the dressing. Adjust the consistency with more water if needed.
4. Pour the Lemon-Tahini Dressing over the salad ingredients in the mixing bowl. Toss gently until everything is evenly coated with the dressing.
5. Taste and adjust seasoning if needed.
6. Serve the Quinoa and Avocado Salad with Lemon-Tahini Dressing immediately, or chill it in the refrigerator for at least 30 minutes before serving to allow the flavors to meld together.
7. Enjoy your refreshing and nutritious salad!

Mediterranean Cucumber Salad with Yogurt Dressing

Ingredients:

For the Salad:

- 2 English cucumbers, thinly sliced
- 1 cup cherry tomatoes, halved
- 1/4 cup red onion, thinly sliced
- 1/4 cup pitted Kalamata olives, halved
- 2 tablespoons chopped fresh parsley
- 2 tablespoons chopped fresh dill
- Salt and pepper to taste

For the Yogurt Dressing:

- 1 cup Greek yogurt
- 2 tablespoons extra virgin olive oil
- 2 tablespoons fresh lemon juice
- 1 clove garlic, minced
- 1 teaspoon dried oregano
- Salt and pepper to taste

Instructions:

1. In a large mixing bowl, combine the thinly sliced cucumbers, halved cherry tomatoes, thinly sliced red onion, halved Kalamata olives, chopped fresh parsley, and chopped fresh dill.
2. In a separate bowl, whisk together the Greek yogurt, extra virgin olive oil, fresh lemon juice, minced garlic, dried oregano, salt, and pepper to make the dressing.
3. Pour the Yogurt Dressing over the salad ingredients in the mixing bowl. Toss gently until everything is evenly coated with the dressing.
4. Taste and adjust seasoning if needed.
5. Serve the Mediterranean Cucumber Salad with Yogurt Dressing immediately, or chill it in the refrigerator for at least 30 minutes before serving to allow the flavors to meld together.
6. Enjoy your refreshing and flavorful salad!

Chicken and Artichoke Salad with White Beans

Ingredients:

For the Salad:

- 2 boneless, skinless chicken breasts
- Salt and pepper to taste
- 1 can (15 ounces) white beans, drained and rinsed
- 1 can (14 ounces) artichoke hearts, drained and quartered
- 1 cup cherry tomatoes, halved
- 1/4 cup red onion, thinly sliced
- 2 tablespoons chopped fresh parsley
- 2 tablespoons chopped fresh basil
- 1/4 cup crumbled feta cheese (optional)

For the Dressing:

- 1/4 cup extra virgin olive oil
- 2 tablespoons white wine vinegar
- 1 clove garlic, minced
- 1 teaspoon Dijon mustard
- 1 teaspoon honey
- Salt and pepper to taste

Instructions:

1. Season the chicken breasts with salt and pepper. Grill or cook them in a skillet over medium-high heat until cooked through, about 6-8 minutes per side. Let them cool, then slice them into strips.
2. In a large mixing bowl, combine the sliced chicken breast strips, white beans, artichoke hearts, halved cherry tomatoes, thinly sliced red onion, chopped fresh parsley, and chopped fresh basil. If using, add the crumbled feta cheese.
3. In a small bowl, whisk together the extra virgin olive oil, white wine vinegar, minced garlic, Dijon mustard, honey, salt, and pepper to make the dressing.

4. Pour the dressing over the salad ingredients in the mixing bowl. Toss gently until everything is evenly coated with the dressing.
5. Taste and adjust seasoning if needed.
6. Serve the Chicken and Artichoke Salad with White Beans immediately, or chill it in the refrigerator for at least 30 minutes before serving to allow the flavors to meld together.
7. Enjoy your delicious and protein-packed salad!

Greek-style Pork and Olive Salad

Ingredients:

For the Pork:

- 1 pound pork tenderloin, thinly sliced
- 2 tablespoons olive oil
- 2 cloves garlic, minced
- 1 teaspoon dried oregano
- Salt and pepper to taste

For the Salad:

- 4 cups mixed salad greens (such as romaine, spinach, or arugula)
- 1 cucumber, sliced
- 1 cup cherry tomatoes, halved
- 1/4 cup red onion, thinly sliced
- 1/4 cup pitted Kalamata olives
- 1/4 cup crumbled feta cheese

For the Dressing:

- 1/4 cup extra virgin olive oil
- 2 tablespoons red wine vinegar
- 1 clove garlic, minced
- 1 teaspoon Dijon mustard
- 1 teaspoon dried oregano
- Salt and pepper to taste

Instructions:

1. In a bowl, combine the olive oil, minced garlic, dried oregano, salt, and pepper. Add the thinly sliced pork tenderloin to the bowl and toss until evenly coated. Let the pork marinate for about 15-30 minutes.

2. Heat a skillet or grill pan over medium-high heat. Cook the marinated pork slices for 3-4 minutes per side, or until they are cooked through and golden brown. Remove from heat and let them rest for a few minutes.
3. In a large mixing bowl, combine the mixed salad greens, sliced cucumber, halved cherry tomatoes, thinly sliced red onion, pitted Kalamata olives, and crumbled feta cheese.
4. In a small bowl, whisk together the extra virgin olive oil, red wine vinegar, minced garlic, Dijon mustard, dried oregano, salt, and pepper to make the dressing.
5. Pour the dressing over the salad ingredients in the mixing bowl. Toss gently until everything is evenly coated with the dressing.
6. Divide the salad among serving plates.
7. Top each serving with the cooked pork slices.
8. Serve the Greek-style Pork and Olive Salad immediately.
9. Enjoy your flavorful and nutritious salad!

Lentil and Salmon Salad with Dill Dressing

Ingredients:

For the Salad:

- 1 cup green lentils, rinsed
- 2 cups water or vegetable broth
- 2 salmon fillets (about 6 ounces each)
- 2 tablespoons olive oil
- Salt and pepper to taste
- 4 cups mixed salad greens (such as spinach, arugula, or romaine)
- 1 cucumber, diced
- 1 cup cherry tomatoes, halved
- 1/4 cup red onion, thinly sliced
- 1/4 cup chopped fresh dill

For the Dill Dressing:

- 1/4 cup extra virgin olive oil
- 2 tablespoons white wine vinegar
- 1 tablespoon fresh lemon juice
- 1 clove garlic, minced
- 1 tablespoon Dijon mustard
- 2 tablespoons chopped fresh dill
- Salt and pepper to taste

Instructions:

1. In a medium saucepan, bring the water or vegetable broth to a boil. Stir in the lentils, cover, and reduce the heat to low. Simmer for 15-20 minutes, or until the lentils are tender but still hold their shape. Drain any excess water and let the lentils cool.
2. Preheat your oven to 400°F (200°C). Place the salmon fillets on a baking sheet lined with parchment paper or aluminum foil. Drizzle with olive oil and season

with salt and pepper to taste. Bake in the preheated oven for 12-15 minutes, or until the salmon is cooked through and flakes easily with a fork. Remove from the oven and let them cool slightly.
3. In a large mixing bowl, combine the cooked and cooled lentils, mixed salad greens, diced cucumber, halved cherry tomatoes, thinly sliced red onion, and chopped fresh dill.
4. In a small bowl, whisk together the extra virgin olive oil, white wine vinegar, fresh lemon juice, minced garlic, Dijon mustard, chopped fresh dill, salt, and pepper to make the dressing.
5. Pour the Dill Dressing over the salad ingredients in the mixing bowl. Toss gently until everything is evenly coated with the dressing.
6. Divide the salad among serving plates.
7. Top each serving with a baked salmon fillet.
8. Serve the Lentil and Salmon Salad with Dill Dressing immediately.
9. Enjoy your flavorful and nutritious salad!

Mediterranean Barley Salad with Grilled Vegetables

Ingredients:

For the Barley Salad:

- 1 cup barley
- 2 cups water or vegetable broth
- 1 medium zucchini, sliced lengthwise
- 1 medium yellow squash, sliced lengthwise
- 1 red bell pepper, seeded and quartered
- 1 yellow bell pepper, seeded and quartered
- 1 red onion, peeled and sliced into thick rounds
- 1 cup cherry tomatoes, halved
- 1/4 cup pitted Kalamata olives, halved
- 1/4 cup crumbled feta cheese
- 2 tablespoons chopped fresh parsley
- 2 tablespoons chopped fresh mint
- Salt and pepper to taste
- Olive oil for grilling

For the Dressing:

- 1/4 cup extra virgin olive oil
- 2 tablespoons red wine vinegar
- 1 clove garlic, minced
- 1 teaspoon Dijon mustard
- 1 teaspoon dried oregano
- Salt and pepper to taste

Instructions:

1. Rinse the barley under cold water in a fine-mesh sieve.

2. In a medium saucepan, bring the water or vegetable broth to a boil. Stir in the barley, cover, and reduce the heat to low. Simmer for 30-40 minutes, or until the barley is tender and has absorbed all the liquid. Remove from heat and let it cool.
3. Preheat your grill or grill pan over medium-high heat.
4. Brush the sliced zucchini, yellow squash, red bell pepper, yellow bell pepper, and red onion rounds with olive oil. Season with salt and pepper.
5. Grill the vegetables for 3-4 minutes per side, or until they are tender and have grill marks. Remove from the grill and let them cool slightly.
6. In a large mixing bowl, combine the cooked and cooled barley, grilled vegetables, halved cherry tomatoes, halved Kalamata olives, crumbled feta cheese, chopped fresh parsley, and chopped fresh mint.
7. In a small bowl, whisk together the extra virgin olive oil, red wine vinegar, minced garlic, Dijon mustard, dried oregano, salt, and pepper to make the dressing.
8. Pour the dressing over the salad ingredients in the mixing bowl. Toss gently until everything is evenly coated with the dressing.
9. Taste and adjust seasoning if needed.
10. Serve the Mediterranean Barley Salad with Grilled Vegetables immediately, or chill it in the refrigerator for at least 30 minutes before serving to allow the flavors to meld together.
11. Enjoy your flavorful and nutritious salad!

Greek-style Turkey and Quinoa Salad

Ingredients:

For the Salad:

- 1 cup quinoa
- 2 cups water or vegetable broth
- 1 pound ground turkey
- 2 tablespoons olive oil
- 2 cloves garlic, minced
- 1 teaspoon dried oregano
- Salt and pepper to taste
- 1 cup cherry tomatoes, halved
- 1/2 English cucumber, diced
- 1/4 cup red onion, finely chopped
- 1/4 cup pitted Kalamata olives, halved
- 1/4 cup crumbled feta cheese
- 2 tablespoons chopped fresh parsley
- 2 tablespoons chopped fresh dill

For the Dressing:

- 1/4 cup extra virgin olive oil
- 2 tablespoons red wine vinegar
- 1 clove garlic, minced
- 1 teaspoon Dijon mustard
- 1 teaspoon dried oregano
- Salt and pepper to taste

Instructions:

1. Rinse the quinoa under cold water in a fine-mesh sieve.

2. In a medium saucepan, bring the water or vegetable broth to a boil. Stir in the quinoa, cover, and reduce the heat to low. Simmer for 15-20 minutes, or until the quinoa is cooked and the liquid is absorbed. Remove from heat and let it cool.
3. In a skillet, heat olive oil over medium heat. Add minced garlic and cook until fragrant, about 1 minute. Add ground turkey, dried oregano, salt, and pepper. Cook until the turkey is browned and cooked through, breaking it up with a spoon as it cooks. Remove from heat and let it cool.
4. In a large mixing bowl, combine the cooked and cooled quinoa, cooked ground turkey, halved cherry tomatoes, diced cucumber, finely chopped red onion, halved Kalamata olives, crumbled feta cheese, chopped fresh parsley, and chopped fresh dill.
5. In a small bowl, whisk together the extra virgin olive oil, red wine vinegar, minced garlic, Dijon mustard, dried oregano, salt, and pepper to make the dressing.
6. Pour the dressing over the salad ingredients in the mixing bowl. Toss gently until everything is evenly coated with the dressing.
7. Taste and adjust seasoning if needed.
8. Serve the Greek-style Turkey and Quinoa Salad immediately, or chill it in the refrigerator for at least 30 minutes before serving to allow the flavors to meld together.
9. Enjoy your flavorful and protein-packed salad!

Quinoa and Chickpea Salad with Roasted Red Pepper Dressing

Ingredients:

For the Salad:

- 1 cup quinoa
- 2 cups water or vegetable broth
- 1 can (15 ounces) chickpeas, drained and rinsed
- 1 cup cherry tomatoes, halved
- 1/2 English cucumber, diced
- 1/4 cup red onion, finely chopped
- 1/4 cup chopped fresh parsley
- Salt and pepper to taste

For the Roasted Red Pepper Dressing:

- 1 large red bell pepper
- 2 tablespoons olive oil
- 1 tablespoon balsamic vinegar
- 1 clove garlic, minced
- 1 teaspoon honey or maple syrup
- Salt and pepper to taste

Instructions:

1. Preheat your oven to broil.
2. Cut the red bell pepper in half and remove the seeds and stem. Place the pepper halves on a baking sheet lined with aluminum foil, cut side down.
3. Broil the red pepper halves for 8-10 minutes, or until the skins are charred and blistered.
4. Remove the red pepper halves from the oven and transfer them to a bowl. Cover the bowl with plastic wrap and let the peppers steam for 10 minutes. This will make it easier to remove the skins.

5. After steaming, peel off the charred skins from the red pepper halves. Chop the roasted red pepper flesh into smaller pieces.
6. In a blender or food processor, combine the chopped roasted red pepper, olive oil, balsamic vinegar, minced garlic, honey or maple syrup, salt, and pepper. Blend until smooth and well combined. If the dressing is too thick, you can add a little water to thin it out.
7. Rinse the quinoa under cold water in a fine-mesh sieve.
8. In a medium saucepan, bring the water or vegetable broth to a boil. Stir in the quinoa, cover, and reduce the heat to low. Simmer for 15-20 minutes, or until the quinoa is cooked and the liquid is absorbed. Remove from heat and let it cool.
9. In a large mixing bowl, combine the cooked and cooled quinoa, drained and rinsed chickpeas, halved cherry tomatoes, diced cucumber, finely chopped red onion, and chopped fresh parsley.
10. Pour the roasted red pepper dressing over the salad ingredients in the mixing bowl. Toss gently until everything is evenly coated with the dressing.
11. Taste and adjust seasoning if needed.
12. Serve the Quinoa and Chickpea Salad with Roasted Red Pepper Dressing immediately, or chill it in the refrigerator for at least 30 minutes before serving to allow the flavors to meld together.
13. Enjoy your flavorful and nutritious salad!

Mediterranean Roasted Beet Salad with Goat Cheese

Ingredients:

For the Salad:

- 3-4 medium beets, washed and trimmed
- 2 tablespoons olive oil
- Salt and pepper to taste
- 4 cups mixed salad greens (such as arugula, spinach, or spring mix)
- 1/4 cup walnuts, toasted and chopped
- 1/4 cup crumbled goat cheese
- 1/4 cup pomegranate arils (optional)
- 2 tablespoons chopped fresh parsley (optional)

For the Dressing:

- 1/4 cup extra virgin olive oil
- 2 tablespoons balsamic vinegar
- 1 teaspoon Dijon mustard
- 1 teaspoon honey
- Salt and pepper to taste

Instructions:

1. Preheat your oven to 400°F (200°C).
2. Place the washed and trimmed beets on a baking sheet lined with aluminum foil. Drizzle them with olive oil and sprinkle with salt and pepper. Tightly wrap the beets in the foil.
3. Roast the beets in the preheated oven for 45-60 minutes, or until they are tender when pierced with a fork. Remove from the oven and let them cool slightly.
4. Once the beets are cool enough to handle, peel off the skins using your fingers or a knife. Cut the roasted beets into bite-sized cubes or slices.
5. In a small bowl, whisk together the extra virgin olive oil, balsamic vinegar, Dijon mustard, honey, salt, and pepper to make the dressing.

6. In a large mixing bowl, combine the mixed salad greens, roasted beet cubes or slices, toasted and chopped walnuts, crumbled goat cheese, pomegranate arils (if using), and chopped fresh parsley (if using).
7. Pour the dressing over the salad ingredients in the mixing bowl. Toss gently until everything is evenly coated with the dressing.
8. Taste and adjust seasoning if needed.
9. Serve the Mediterranean Roasted Beet Salad with Goat Cheese immediately.
10. Enjoy your colorful and flavorful salad!

Grilled Tofu and Vegetable Salad with Feta

Ingredients:

For the Grilled Tofu:

- 1 block (14-16 ounces) firm tofu, drained and pressed
- 2 tablespoons soy sauce
- 1 tablespoon olive oil
- 1 clove garlic, minced
- 1 teaspoon grated ginger
- Salt and pepper to taste

For the Grilled Vegetables:

- 1 red bell pepper, seeded and sliced
- 1 yellow bell pepper, seeded and sliced
- 1 zucchini, sliced lengthwise
- 1 yellow squash, sliced lengthwise
- 1 red onion, peeled and sliced into thick rounds
- 2 tablespoons olive oil
- Salt and pepper to taste

For the Salad:

- 4 cups mixed salad greens (such as spinach, arugula, or romaine)
- 1/4 cup sliced Kalamata olives
- 1/4 cup crumbled feta cheese
- 2 tablespoons chopped fresh parsley
- 2 tablespoons chopped fresh mint

For the Dressing:

- 1/4 cup extra virgin olive oil
- 2 tablespoons balsamic vinegar
- 1 clove garlic, minced
- 1 teaspoon Dijon mustard

- Salt and pepper to taste

Instructions:

1. Start by preparing the tofu. Cut the pressed tofu into cubes or slices, depending on your preference.
2. In a shallow dish, whisk together the soy sauce, olive oil, minced garlic, grated ginger, salt, and pepper. Add the tofu cubes or slices to the marinade and let them marinate for at least 30 minutes.
3. Preheat your grill or grill pan over medium-high heat.
4. In a large mixing bowl, toss the sliced red bell pepper, yellow bell pepper, zucchini, yellow squash, and red onion with olive oil, salt, and pepper until evenly coated.
5. Grill the marinated tofu and prepared vegetables for 3-4 minutes per side, or until they are tender and have grill marks. Remove from the grill and let them cool slightly.
6. In a separate small bowl, whisk together the extra virgin olive oil, balsamic vinegar, minced garlic, Dijon mustard, salt, and pepper to make the dressing.
7. In a large mixing bowl, combine the mixed salad greens, sliced Kalamata olives, crumbled feta cheese, chopped fresh parsley, and chopped fresh mint.
8. Add the grilled tofu and vegetables to the salad ingredients in the mixing bowl.
9. Pour the dressing over the salad ingredients. Toss gently until everything is evenly coated with the dressing.
10. Taste and adjust seasoning if needed.
11. Serve the Grilled Tofu and Vegetable Salad with Feta immediately.
12. Enjoy your flavorful and nutritious salad!

Greek-style Chicken and Pasta Salad

Ingredients:

For the Salad:

- 8 ounces pasta (such as penne or fusilli)
- 2 boneless, skinless chicken breasts
- 2 tablespoons olive oil
- 2 cloves garlic, minced
- 1 teaspoon dried oregano
- Salt and pepper to taste
- 1 cup cherry tomatoes, halved
- 1/2 English cucumber, diced
- 1/4 cup red onion, finely chopped
- 1/4 cup pitted Kalamata olives, halved
- 1/4 cup crumbled feta cheese
- 2 tablespoons chopped fresh parsley
- 2 tablespoons chopped fresh dill

For the Dressing:

- 1/4 cup extra virgin olive oil
- 2 tablespoons red wine vinegar
- 1 clove garlic, minced
- 1 teaspoon Dijon mustard
- 1 teaspoon dried oregano
- Salt and pepper to taste

Instructions:

1. Cook the pasta according to the package instructions until al dente. Drain and rinse under cold water to stop the cooking process. Set aside.
2. Preheat your grill or grill pan over medium-high heat.

3. Season the chicken breasts with olive oil, minced garlic, dried oregano, salt, and pepper.
4. Grill the chicken breasts for about 6-8 minutes per side, or until cooked through and no longer pink in the center. Remove from heat and let them rest for a few minutes before slicing them into strips.
5. In a large mixing bowl, combine the cooked pasta, sliced grilled chicken breast strips, halved cherry tomatoes, diced cucumber, finely chopped red onion, halved Kalamata olives, crumbled feta cheese, chopped fresh parsley, and chopped fresh dill.
6. In a small bowl, whisk together the extra virgin olive oil, red wine vinegar, minced garlic, Dijon mustard, dried oregano, salt, and pepper to make the dressing.
7. Pour the dressing over the salad ingredients in the mixing bowl. Toss gently until everything is evenly coated with the dressing.
8. Taste and adjust seasoning if needed.
9. Serve the Greek-style Chicken and Pasta Salad immediately, or chill it in the refrigerator for at least 30 minutes before serving to allow the flavors to meld together.
10. Enjoy your flavorful and satisfying salad!

Lentil and Tofu Salad with Lemon-Tahini Dressing

Ingredients:

For the Salad:

- 1 cup green or brown lentils, rinsed
- 2 cups water or vegetable broth
- 1 block (14-16 ounces) firm tofu, drained and pressed
- 2 tablespoons olive oil
- Salt and pepper to taste
- 4 cups mixed salad greens (such as spinach, arugula, or spring mix)
- 1/2 cucumber, diced
- 1/2 cup cherry tomatoes, halved
- 1/4 cup red onion, thinly sliced
- 1/4 cup chopped fresh parsley
- 1/4 cup chopped fresh cilantro (optional)
- 2 tablespoons toasted sesame seeds (optional)

For the Lemon-Tahini Dressing:

- 1/4 cup tahini
- 1/4 cup water
- 2 tablespoons fresh lemon juice
- 1 tablespoon olive oil
- 1 clove garlic, minced
- 1 teaspoon honey or maple syrup
- 1/2 teaspoon ground cumin
- Salt and pepper to taste

Instructions:

1. In a medium saucepan, bring the water or vegetable broth to a boil. Add the rinsed lentils and reduce heat to low. Simmer for 20-25 minutes, or until the

lentils are tender but still hold their shape. Drain any excess liquid and let the lentils cool.
2. While the lentils are cooking, prepare the tofu. Cut the pressed tofu into cubes or slices.
3. Heat 2 tablespoons of olive oil in a skillet over medium heat. Add the tofu cubes or slices to the skillet and season with salt and pepper. Cook for 4-5 minutes on each side, or until golden brown and crispy. Remove from heat and let them cool slightly.
4. In a large mixing bowl, combine the cooked and cooled lentils, cooked tofu, mixed salad greens, diced cucumber, halved cherry tomatoes, thinly sliced red onion, chopped fresh parsley, chopped fresh cilantro (if using), and toasted sesame seeds (if using).
5. In a small bowl, whisk together the tahini, water, fresh lemon juice, olive oil, minced garlic, honey or maple syrup, ground cumin, salt, and pepper to make the Lemon-Tahini Dressing.
6. Pour the dressing over the salad ingredients in the mixing bowl. Toss gently until everything is evenly coated with the dressing.
7. Taste and adjust seasoning if needed.
8. Serve the Lentil and Tofu Salad with Lemon-Tahini Dressing immediately, or chill it in the refrigerator for at least 30 minutes before serving to allow the flavors to meld together.
9. Enjoy your protein-packed and flavorful salad!